A HymnTune Psalter

Book One

Gradual Psalms: Advent through the Day of Pentecost

Revised Common Lectionary Edition

Carl P. Daw, Jr. and Kevin R. Hackett

CHURCH PUBLISHING INCORPORATED

Church Publishing Incorporated
19 East 34th Street
New York, NY 10016

CONTENTS

INTRODUCTION

The Psalms are the hymns of ancient Israel. In them, every mood and emotion of the human heart is given voice, from the heights and ecstasy of praise to the depths and darkness of despair. While the texts of Israel's hymns have survived, sadly, the music has not. We can only imagine the rugged marching tune that must have carried a wilderness psalm like Psalm 107 or the delicate, homespun melody to which Psalm 131 must surely have been hummed or the protest song to which Psalm 137 was defiantly sung. Certainly, they must have been tunes that were much loved by the people, and certainly they must have been known by heart.

The early Christian church, springing as it did from Jewish soil, naturally continued the tradition of offering its life to God in song through the prayer and praise of the psalms (which, being hymns, were meant to be sung). Thanks to the eventual development of a convention like standard musical notation, we retain some vestiges of this ancient tradition and its evolution. Plainsong melodies, some of which may be traceable to ancient Jewish origins, have conveyed to us (with Latin texts) a priceless body of Judeo-Christian song. Subsequently, at the Reformation the concern that the sacred texts of the Church be available to ordinary people in the vernacular resulted in two significant developments: Latin chant texts were translated into English, and the melodies adapted to fit; and metrical versions of the psalms (precursors of the modern hymn) gained broad popularity. A further refinement of the chant resulted in the 18th-century development of what is now known as Anglican chant, facilitating the singing of non-metrical translations of the psalms.

Beautiful as plainsong is, however, it is an idiom whose modal tonalities and unfamiliar cadences are foreign to the sensibilities and beyond the capability of many modern worshipers. Anglican chant (even in its simplified form) relies on skillful choral leadership and is inaccessible to many Episcopal congregations. And metrical psalmody, undeniably useful in many settings, is one more step removed from the original text.

This psalter draws upon much of what has gone before; indeed, this collection does not attempt to create a new manner of singing the psalms. Rather, it endeavors to draw together various traditions of psalmody by preserving the refrain/verse pattern of Israel's worship (the responsorial form); by using a hybrid form of the chant (simplified Anglican chant, itself a hybrid of plainsong); and most significantly, by basing its refrains on hymn tunes (many of which carried the texts of early metrical psalms) likely to be already known by heart by most Protestants in North America.

As a general strategy for recovering the experience of the psalms as sung scripture, it seemed fitting that these ancient hymns should be wedded in our day to the hymn tunes that have become familiar in Christian worship. But more particularly, *A HymnTune Psalter* is offered as a pastoral resource for those responsible for planning and leading the Church's worship in congregations that may have felt unable to sing the psalms in any of the available styles. Through the use of varied antiphon tunes and chant tones, it also attempts to convey the distinctive character of each psalm and provides an alternative to the unexpressive monotony of singing every psalm to one or two simplified Anglican chants. By drawing on the hymn melodies already known to them, the congregation can recognize and recover something of the vitality and comprehensiveness of the psalms.

Performance Notes

The translation used in this collection is that of The Book of Common Prayer 1979. The texts of the antiphons are those appointed for each Proper. They are identical to those used in *Gradual Psalms* and in the lectionary-based bulletin inserts used in many congregations. Indeed, given the familiarity of tunes for the antiphons, the availability of the antiphon on the scripture insert may eliminate the need to print the antiphon and its music.

The traditional method for singing this type of psalmody is as follows:

> Cantor or choir sings the antiphon;
> **all repeat.**
>
> Cantor or choir sings the first set of verses;
> **all respond with the antiphon.**

And so forth, always concluding with the antiphon.

The Antiphons

At its best, the antiphon of a psalm is the peoples' "take-home-package," the word of scripture that, set to music and committed to memory, "dwells in the heart richly." The tunes of the antiphons are drawn from familiar hymns found in *The Hymnal 1982*. All are in the public domain and most are part of the larger Church's standard repertoire. Wherever possible, tunes traditionally associated with a metrical version of particular psalm (e.g., Psalm 46 and *Ein feste Burg*), have been used as a means of reinforcing that association. Other rationales for tune selections include seasonal associations (e.g., *Easter Hymn*), thematic connections with tune names or texts (e.g., *Light* for Psalm 27), and the necessity of accommodating the sometimes erratic stress patterns of the appointed antiphon. In many cases, it will be appropriate and desirable that the hymn on which the antiphon is based be used in the same liturgical celebration.

In performance, the tempo and accompaniment (if any) of the antiphon should generally approximate that of the tune on which it is based. In some cases, however, in order to accommodate a wordier text, a slightly broader tempo will be in order. Like *The Hymnal 1982*, this psalter provides only a melody line for antiphons intended to be sung in unison and full harmony for those to be sung in parts. If the antiphons are accompanied, it is important that organ registrations or other instrumental accompaniment be chosen that will support and encourage congregational singing.

The Verses and Chant Tones

The chant tones in this psalter are cast as simplified Anglican chant. Each tone features two four-chord progressions (designated A and B). One four-chord sequence usually carries the text of an entire verse. The first and third chords in each progression are reciting chords, and the second and fourth chords function as medial and final cadences. We have avoided slavish adherence to the practice of changing chords on the last word or syllable of a line, opting occasionally to vary the formula in order to convey the meaning more effectively (e.g., Psalm 118:23a, "This is the **Lord's doing**" rather than "This is the Lord's **doing**" or worse, "This is the Lord's do**ing**."). When inner voices have a second note in a cadential chord, it should be reserved for the final syllable if there are more than one or for the second beat of a single sustained syllable.

The customary pattern of singing two psalm verses between antiphons means that the first verse is sung to part A of the chant tone and the second verse to part B. Where the sentence structure or poetic patterns require it, more than two verses may sometimes be sung before an antiphon. In these cases the pattern of singing the first half twice (i.e., AAB) or of singing the full chant tone twice (ABAB) will be marked in the left-hand margin. Similarly, a very long verse may sometimes need to be subdivided and sung to the full chant tone rather than to half of it. In such cases the verse is printed as four lines of text and is sung in the customary AB pattern.

The verses may be chanted in a variety of ways. Ideally, they would be sung unaccompanied in four-part harmony by a quartet or choir. The antiphon may then be accompanied or not, depending on the confidence and skill of the congregation. Alternatively, a solo voice accompanied by an organ, piano, autoharp, or other chordal instrument can provide satisfying leadership for the verses. If possible, some variation from the instrumentation for the antiphon (e.g., change of organ registration or the addition of handbells) would be desirable. To ensure a smooth transition between the verse and the antiphon, a slight elongation of the word or syllable at each cadence will effect a sense of pulse for the congregation and will help to cue their entrance.

Making Copies for Congregational Use

Purchase of this volume carries with it an authorization for congregations to reproduce in service leaflets either the antiphon or the entire setting, as appropriate. Versions of the antiphons suitable for photocopying can be found at the end of this volume, or the antiphons may be downloaded free of charge in EPS or TIF format at **http://www.churchpublishing.org/hymntunepsalterbookone**

Regardless of the source from which the antiphon or entire setting is taken, the following copyright notice must be included on each copy:

Acknowledgments

In the course of preparing the original version and the current revision of this psalter, we have been encouraged and helped by many people, and we welcome the opportunity to express our appreciation to them. The initial positive response to a very sketchy proposal came from Frank Hemlin, and we were grateful for his early assurance that Church Publishing would be interested and for continuing support in the long transition from good idea to actual publication. As the project proceeded, various groups used portions of these materials in order to evaluate their viability, especially the Community of Celebration in Aliquippa, Pennsylvania, and the Society of Saint John the Evangelist in Cambridge, Massachusetts. We are especially indebted to Dr. William Bradley Roberts and the people of St. Philip's in the Hills, Tucson, Arizona, for extended use and much affirmation.

In the preparation for printing, we have been carefully and supportively guided by Marilyn Haskel and Frank Tedeschi of Church Publishing. In this final phase, as throughout its earlier stages, May Bates Daw has been an invaluable source of sound advice and an unfailing support.

Carl P. Daw, Jr.
Kevin R. Hackett, SSJE

Year A

RCL Advent 1A Psalm 122

based on "Helmsley" (H82–57)

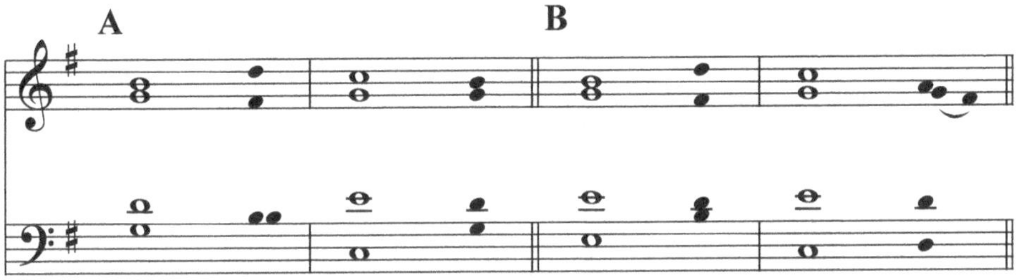

2 Now our feet are standing *
   within your gates, O Jerusalem.
3 Jerusalem is built as a city *
   that is at unity with itself; [ANT.]

4 To which the tribes go up,
the tribes of the LORD, *
   the assembly of Israel,
   to praise the Name of the LORD.
5 For there are the thrones of judgment, *
   the thrones of the house of David. [ANT.]

6 Pray for the peace of Jerusalem: *
   "May they prosper who love you.
7 Peace be within your walls *
   and quietness within your towers. [ANT.]

8 For my brethren and companions' sake, *
   I pray for your prosperity.
9 Because of the house of the Lord our God, *
   I will seek to do you good." [ANT.]

RCL Advent 2A Psalm 72: 1–8, 18–19

based on "Es flog ein kleins Waldvögelein" (H82–616)

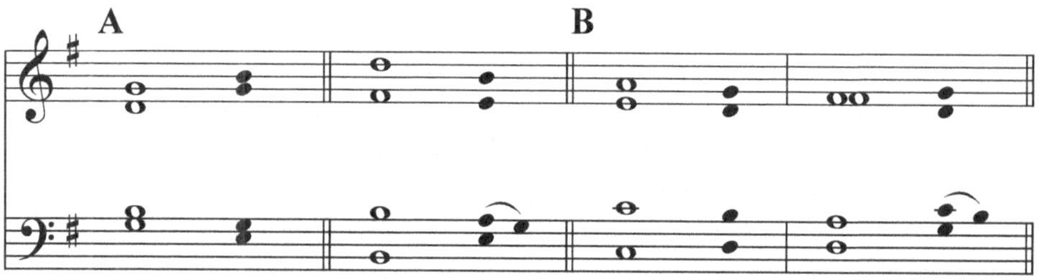

A 1 Give the King your justice, O God, *
and your righteousness to the King's Son;
A 2 That he may rule your people righteously *
and the poor with justice;
B 3 That the mountains may bring prosperity to the people, *
and the little hills bring righteousness. [ANT.]

4 He shall defend the needy among the people; *
he shall rescue the poor and crush the oppressor.
5 He shall live as long as the sun and moon endure, *
from one generation to another. [ANT.]

A 6 He shall come down like rain upon the mown field, *
like showers that water the earth.
A 7 In his time shall the righteous flourish; *
there shall be abundance of peace till the moon shall be no more.
B 8 He shall rule from sea to sea, *
and from the River to the ends of the earth. [ANT.]

18 Blessed be the Lord God, the God of Israel, *
who alone does wondrous deeds!
19 And blessed be his glorious Name for ever! *
and may all the earth be filled with his glory.
Amen. Amen. [ANT.]

RCL Advent 3A   Psalm 146: 4–9

based on "Nun komm, der Heiden Heiland" (H82–54)

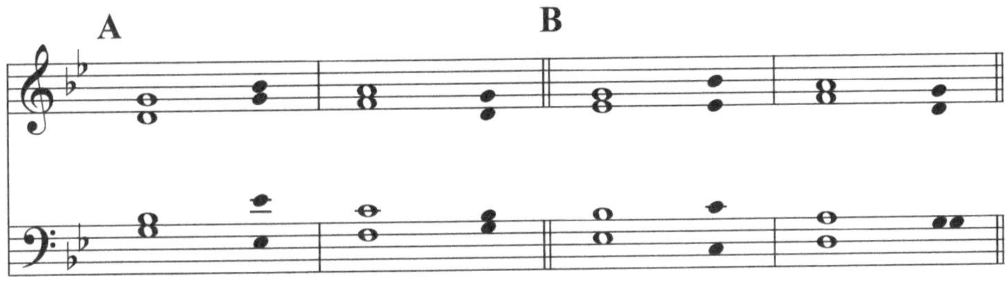

A 4 Happy are they who have the God of Jacob for their help! *
whose hope is in the LORD their God;
A 5 Who made heaven and earth, the seas, and all that is in them; *
who keeps his promise for ever;
B 6 Who gives justice to those who are oppressed, *
and food to those who hunger. [ANT.]

A 7 The LORD sets the prisoners free;
the LORD opens the eyes of the blind; *
the LORD lifts up those who are bowed down;
A 8 The LORD loves the righteous;
the LORD cares for the stranger; *
he sustains the orphan and widow,
but frustrates the way of the wicked.
B 9 The LORD shall reign for ever, *
your God, O Zion, throughout all generations.
Hallelujah! [ANT.]

RCL Advent 3A Canticle 15

based on "Birmingham" (H82–437)

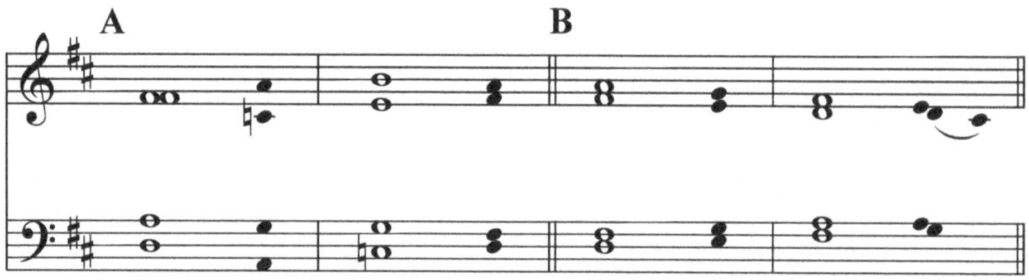

1 My soul proclaims the greatness of the Lord,
my spirit rejoices in God my Savior, *
for he has looked with favor on his lowly servant.
2 From this day all generations will call me blessed: *
the Almighty has done great things for me,
and holy is his Name. [ANT.]

3 He has mercy on those who fear him *
in every generation.
4 He has shown the strength of his arm,
he has scattered the proud in their conceit. [ANT.]

5 He has cast down the mighty from their thrones, *
and has lifted up the lowly.
6 He has filled the hungry with good things, *
and the rich he has sent away empty. [ANT.]

7 He has come to the help of his servant Israel, *
for he has remembered his promise of mercy,
8 The promise he has made to our fathers, *
to Abraham and his children for ever. [ANT.]

RCL Advent 4A   Psalm 80: 1–7, 16–18

based on "Birmingham" (H82–437)

A B

1 Hear, O Shepherd of Israel, leading Joseph like a flock; *
  shine forth, you that are enthroned upon the cherubim.
2 In the presence of Ephraim, Benjamin, and Manasseh, *
  stir up your strength and come to help us. [ANT.]

A 4 O LORD God of hosts, *
  how long will you be angered
  despite the prayers of your people?
A 5 You have fed them with the bread of tears; *
  you have given them bowls of tears to drink.
B 6 You have made us the derision of our neighbors, *
  and our enemies laugh us to scorn. [ANT.]

16 Let your hand be upon the man of your right hand, *
  the son of man you have made so strong for yourself.
17 And so will we never turn away from you; *
  give us life, that we may call upon your Name. [ANT.]

For
Christmas
through
Epiphany 1
see
Pages 98–105

RCL Epiphany 2A **Psalm 40: 1–12**

based on "Old 124th" (H82–149)

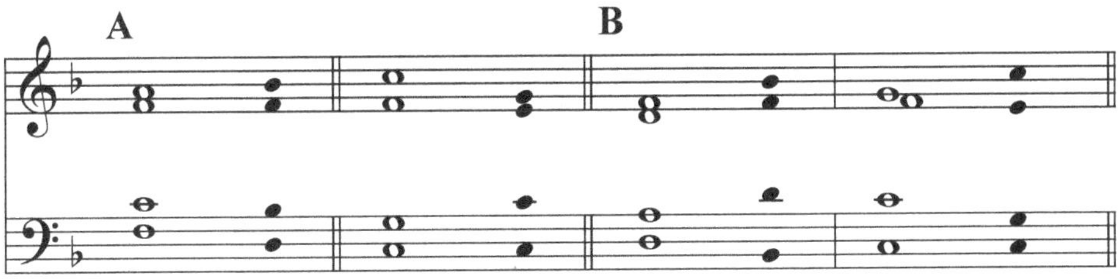

A 1 I waited patiently upon the Lord; *
he stooped to me and heard my cry.
B 2 He lifted me out of the desolate pit, out of the mire and clay; *
he set my feet upon a high cliff and made my footing sure.
A 3 He put a new song in my mouth,
a song of praise to our God; *
many shall see, and stand in awe,
and put their trust in the Lord.
B 4 Happy are they who trust in the Lord! *
they do not resort to evil spirits or turn to false gods. [ANT.]

A 5 Great things are they that you have done, O Lord my God!
how great your wonders and your plans for us! *
there is none who can be compared with you.
B 6 Oh, that I could make them known and tell them! *
but they are more than I can count.
A 7 In sacrifice and offering you take no pleasure *
(you have given me ears to hear you);
B 8 Burnt-offering and sin-offering you have not required, *
and so I said, "Behold, I come. [ANT.]

9 In the roll of the book it is written concerning me: *
'I love to do your will, O my God;
your law is deep in my heart.'"
10 I proclaimed righteousness in the great congregation; *
behold, I did not restrain my lips;
and that, O Lord, you know. [ANT.]

11 Your righteousness have I not hidden in my heart;
I have spoken of your faithfulness and your deliverance; *
I have not concealed your love and faithfulness from the
great congregation.
12 You are the Lord;
do not withhold your compassion from me; *
let your love and your faithfulness keep me safe for ever. [ANT.]

RCL Epiphany 3A Psalm 27: 1, 5–13

based on "Light" (H82–667)

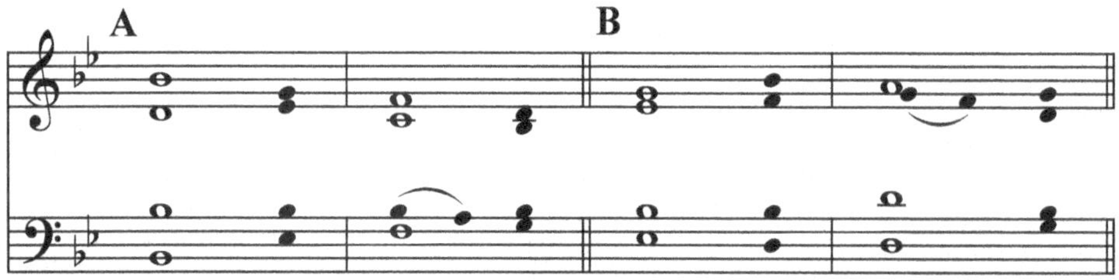

1 The LORD is my light and my salvation;
whom then shall I fear? *
the LORD is the strength of my life;
of whom then shall I be afraid? [ANT.]

5 One thing have I asked of the LORD;
one thing I seek; *
that I may dwell in the house of the LORD all the days of my life;
6 To behold the fair beauty of the LORD *
and to seek him in his temple. [ANT.]

A 7 For in the day of trouble he shall keep me safe in his shelter; *
he shall hide me in the secrecy of his dwelling
and set me high upon a rock.
A 8 Even now he lifts up my head *
above my enemies round about me.
B 9 Therefore I will offer in his dwelling an oblation
with sounds of great gladness; *
I will sing and make music to the LORD. [ANT.]

A 10 Hearken to my voice, O LORD, when I call; *
have mercy on me and answer me.
B 11 You speak in my heart and say, "Seek my face." *
Your face, LORD, will I seek.
A 12 Hide not your face from me, *
nor turn away your servant in displeasure.
B 13 You have been my helper;
cast me not away; *
do not forsake me, O God of my salvation. [ANT.]

For
The Presentation, February 2
see
Page 106 – 107

RCL Epiphany 4A Psalm 15

based on "Festal Song" (H82–551)

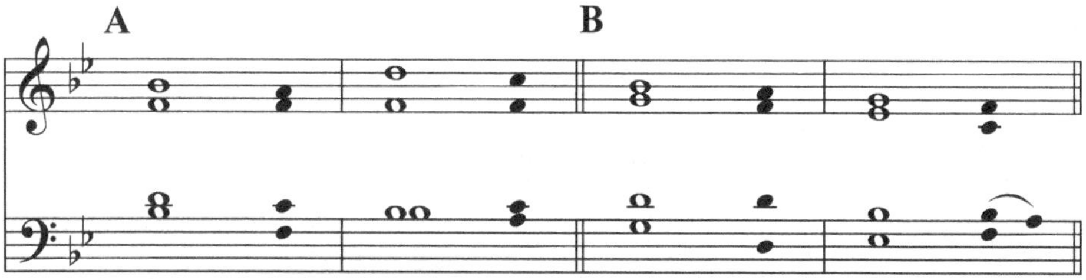

1 LORD, who may dwell in your tabernacle? *
who may abide upon your holy hill?
2 Whoever leads a blameless life and does what is right, *
who speaks the truth from his heart. [ANT.]

3 There is no guile upon his tongue;
he does no evil to his friend; *
he does not heap contempt upon his neighbor.
4 In his sight the wicked is rejected, *
but he honors those who fear the LORD. [ANT.]

A 5 He has sworn to do no wrong *
and does not take back his word.
A 6 He does not give his money in hope of gain, *
nor does he take a bribe against the innocent.
B 7 Whoever does these things *
shall never be overthrown. [ANT.]

RCL Epiphany 5A Psalm 112: 1–9 (10)

based on "O quanta qualia" (H82–348, 623)

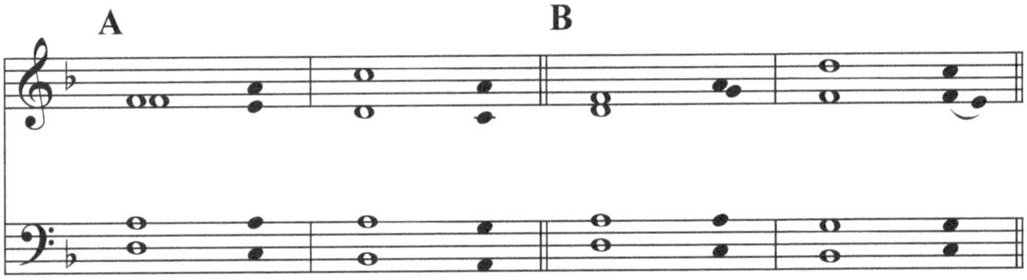

A 1 Hallelujah!
Happy are they who fear the LORD *
and have great delight in his commandments!
A 2 Their descendants will be mighty in the land; *
the generation of the upright will be blessed.
B 3 Wealth and riches will be in their house, *
and their righteousness will last for ever. [ANT.]

A 4 Light shines in the darkness for the upright; *
the righteous are merciful and full of compassion.
A 5 It is good for them to be generous in lending *
and to manage their affairs with justice.
B 6 For they will never be shaken; *
the righteous will be kept in everlasting remembrance. [ANT.]

7 They will not be afraid of any evil rumors; *
their heart is right;
they put their trust in the LORD.
8 Their heart is established and will not shrink, *
until they see their desire upon their enemies. [ANT.]

9 They have given freely to the poor, *
and their righteousness stands fast for ever;
they will hold up their head with honor.
10 The wicked will see it and be angry;
they will gnash their teeth and pine away; *
the desires of the wicked will perish. [ANT.]

RCL Epiphany 6A Psalm 119: 1–8

based on "Hymn to Joy" (H82–376)

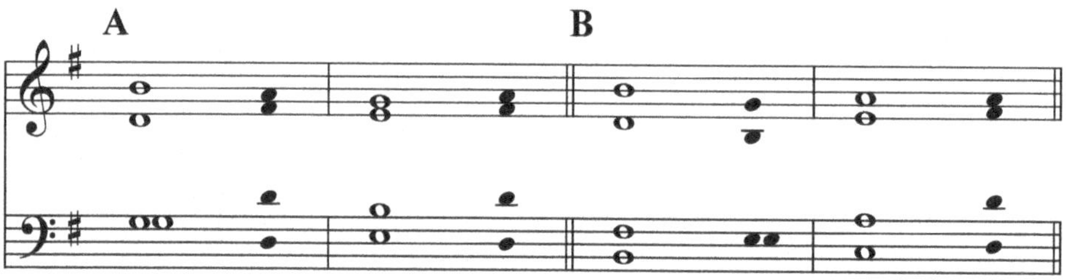

A 1 Happy are they whose way is blameless, *
who walk in the law of the LORD!
A 2 Happy are they who observe his decrees *
and seek him with all their hearts!
B 3 Who never do any wrong, *
but always walk in his ways. [ANT.]

A 4 You laid down your commandments, *
that we should fully keep them.
A 5 Oh, that my ways were made so direct *
that I might keep your statutes!
B 6 Then I should not be put to shame, *
when I regard all your commandments. [ANT.]

7 I will thank you with an unfeigned heart, *
when I have learned your righteous judgments.
8 I will keep your statutes; *
do not utterly forsake me. [ANT.]

RCL Epiphany 7A **Psalm 119: 33–40**

based on "Eventide" (H82–662)

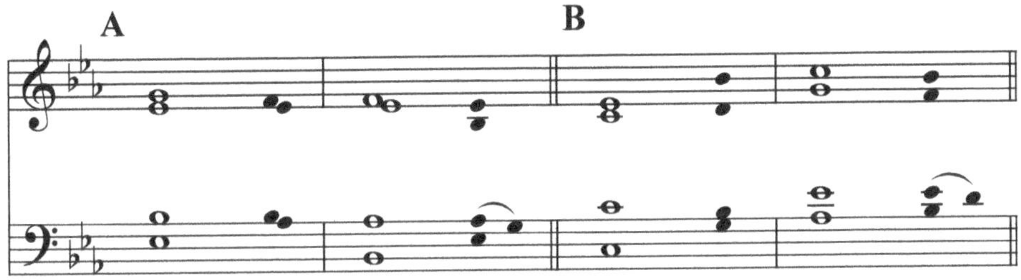

33 Teach me, O LORD, the way of your statutes, *
and I shall keep it to the end.
34 Give me understanding, and I shall keep your law; *
I shall keep it with all my heart. [ANT.]

35 Make me go in the path of your commandments, *
for that is my desire.
36 Incline my heart to your decrees *
and not to unjust gain. [ANT.]

37 Turn my eyes from watching what is worthless; *
give me life in your ways.
38 Fulfill your promise to your servant, *
which you make to those who fear you. [ANT.]

39 Turn away the reproach which I dread, *
because your judgments are good.
40 Behold, I long for your commandments; *
in your righteousness preserve my life. [ANT.]

RCL Epiphany 8A Psalm 131

based on "Picardy" (H82–324)

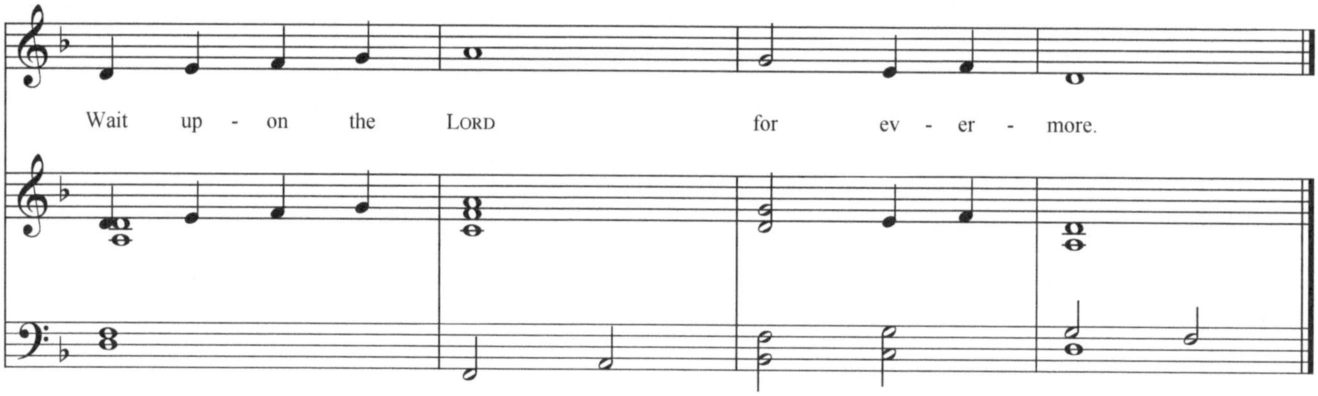

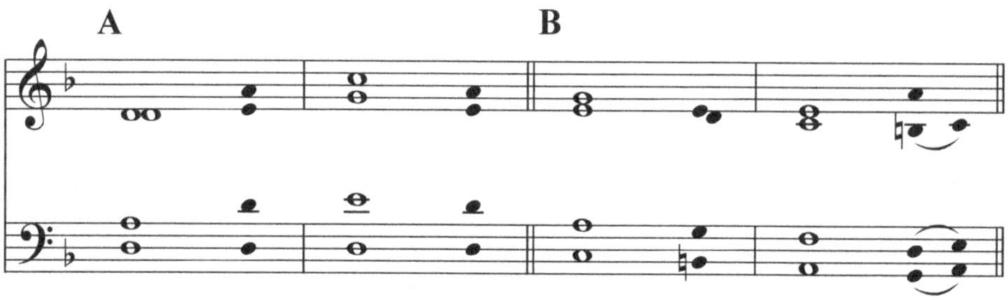

1 O LORD, I am not proud; *
I have no haughty looks.
2 I do not occupy myself with great matters, *
or with things that are too hard for me. [ANT.]

3 But I still my soul and make it quiet,
like a child upon its mother's breast; *
my soul is quieted within me.
4 O Israel, wait upon the LORD, *
from this time forth for evermore. [ANT.]

RCL Epiphany Last A **Psalm 2**

based on "Wareham" (H82–137)

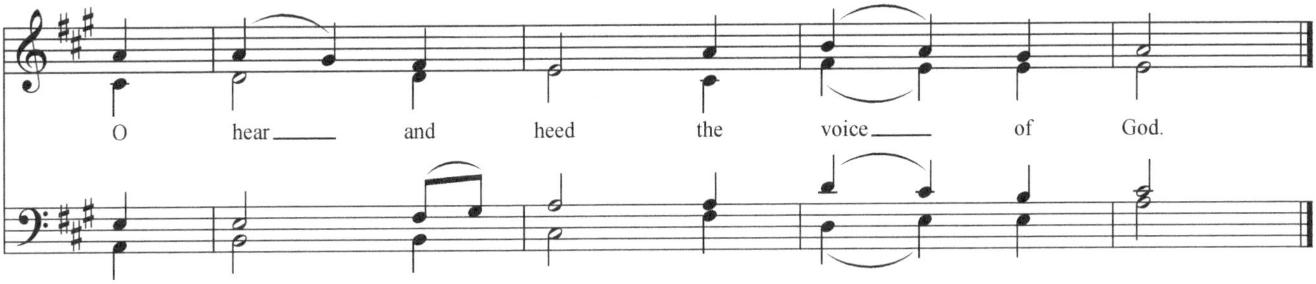

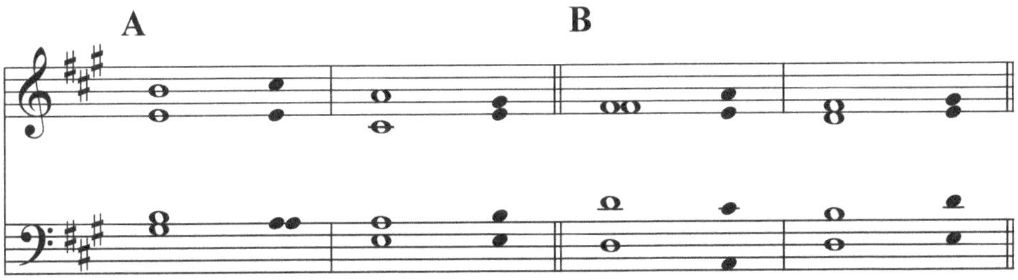

1 Why are the nations in an uproar? *
Why do the peoples mutter empty threats?
2 Why do the kings of the earth rise up in revolt,
and the princes plot together, *
against the LORD and against his Anointed? [ANT.]

A 3 "Let us break their yoke," they say; *
"let us cast off their bonds from us."
A 4 He whose throne is in heaven is laughing; *
the LORD has them in derision.
B 5 Then he speaks to them in his wrath, *
and his rage fills them with terror. [ANT.]

A 6 "I myself have set my king *
upon my holy hill of Zion."
B 7 Let me announce the decree of the LORD: *
he said to me, "You are my Son;
this day have I begotten you.
A 8 Ask of me, and I will give you the nations for
your inheritance *
and the ends of the earth for your possession.
B 9 You shall crush them with an iron rod *
and shatter them like a piece of pottery." [ANT.]

A 10 And now, you kings, be wise; *
be warned, you rulers of the earth.
B 11 Submit to the LORD with fear, *
and with trembling bow before him;
A 12 Lest he be angry and you perish; *
for his wrath is quickly kindled.
B 13 Happy are they all *
who take refuge in him! [ANT.]

RCL Epiphany Last A Psalm 99

based on "Old 124th" (H82–149)

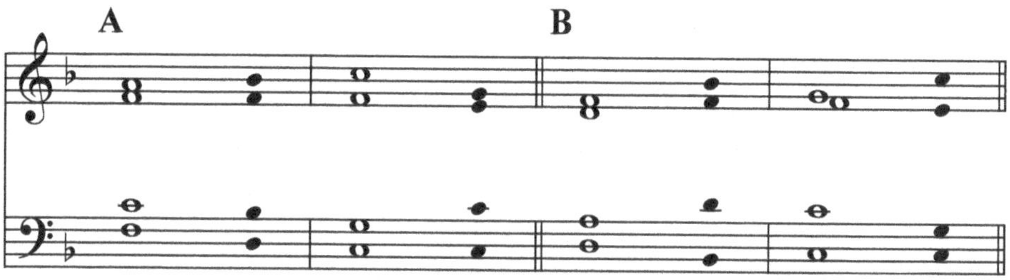

A 1 The LORD is King;
let the people tremble; *
he is enthroned upon the cherubim;
let the earth shake.
A 2 The LORD is great in Zion; *
he is high above all peoples.
B 3 Let them confess his Name, which is great and awesome; *
he is the Holy One. [ANT.]

4 "O mighty King, lover of justice,
you have established equity; *
you have executed justice and righteousness in Jacob."
5 Proclaim the greatness of the LORD our God
and fall down before his footstool; *
he is the Holy One. [ANT.]

6 Moses and Aaron among his priests,
and Samuel among those who call upon his Name, *
they called upon the LORD, and he answered them.
7 He spoke to them out of the pillar of cloud; *
they kept his testimonies and the decree that he gave them. [ANT.]

8 "O LORD our God, you answered them indeed; *
you were a God who forgave them,
yet punished them for their evil deeds."
9 Proclaim the greatness of the LORD our God
and worship him upon his holy hill; *
for the LORD our God is the Holy One. [ANT.]

For

Ash Wednesday

see

Page 108

RCL Lent 1A Psalm 32

based on "Tender Thought" (H82–702)

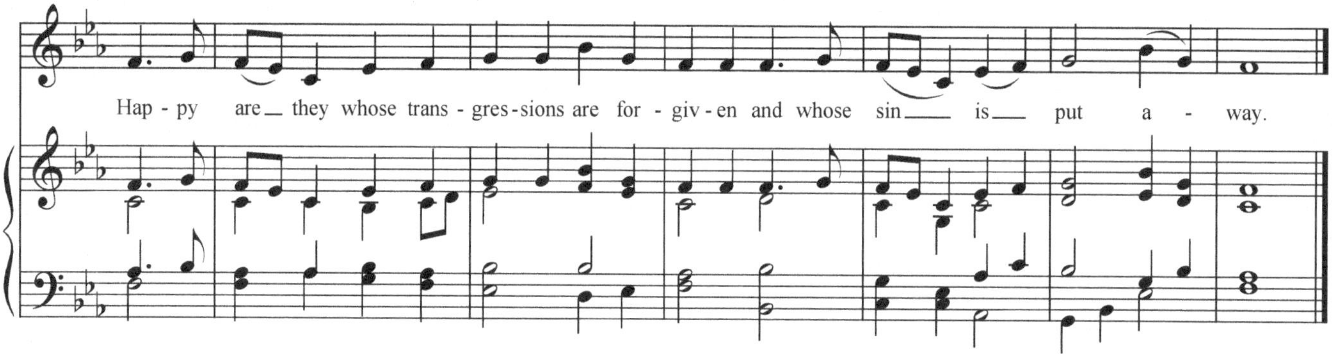

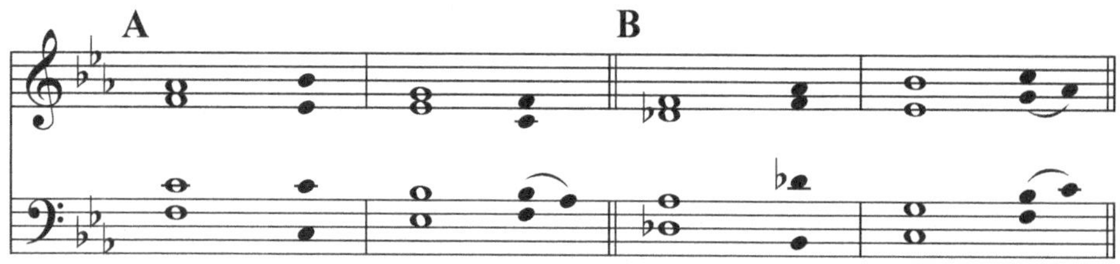

1 Happy are they whose transgressions are forgiven, *
and whose sin is put away!
2 Happy are they to whom the LORD imputes no guilt, *
and in whose spirit there is no guile! [ANT.]

A 3 While I held my tongue, my bones withered away, *
because of my groaning all day long.
B 4 For your hand was heavy upon me day and night; *
my moisture was dried up as in the heat of summer.
A 5 Then I acknowledged my sin to you, *
and did not conceal my guilt.
B 6 I said, "I will confess my transgressions to the LORD." *
Then you forgave me the guilt of my sin. [ANT.]

7 Therefore all the faithful will make their prayers to you in time of trouble; *
when the great waters overflow, they shall not reach them.
8 You are my hiding-place;
you preserve me from trouble; *
you surround me with shouts of deliverance. [ANT.]

9 "I will instruct you and teach you in the way that you should go; *
I will guide you with my eye.
10 Do not be like horse or mule, which have no understanding; *
who must be fitted with bit and bridle,
or else they will not stay near you." [ANT.]

11 Great are the tribulations of the wicked; *
but mercy embraces those who trust in the LORD.
12 Be glad, you righteous, and rejoice in the LORD; *
shout for joy, all who are true of heart. [ANT.]

RCL Lent 2A Psalm 121

based on "Munich" (H82–632)

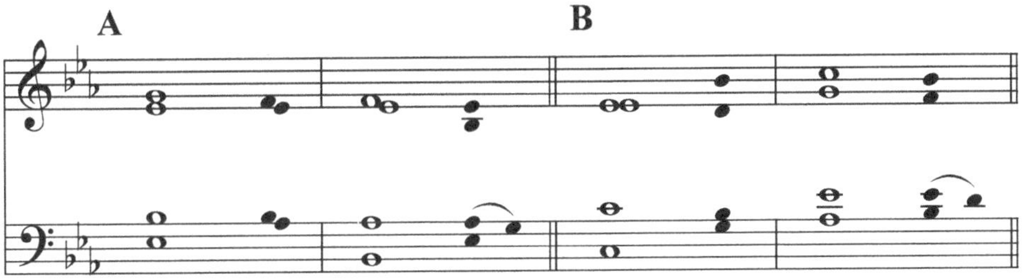

1 I lift up my eyes to the hills; *
from where is my help to come?
2 My help comes from the LORD, *
the maker of heaven and earth. [ANT.]

3 He will not let your foot be moved *
and he who watches over you will not fall asleep.
4 Behold, he who keeps watch over Israel *
shall neither slumber nor sleep; [ANT.]

5 The LORD himself watches over you; *
the LORD is your shade at your right hand,
6 So that the sun shall not strike you by day, *
nor the moon by night. [ANT.]

7 The LORD shall preserve you from all evil; *
it is he who shall keep you safe.
8 The LORD shall watch over your going out and
your coming in, *
from this time forth for evermore. [ANT.]

RCL Lent 3A Psalm 95

based on "Land of Rest" (H82–304)

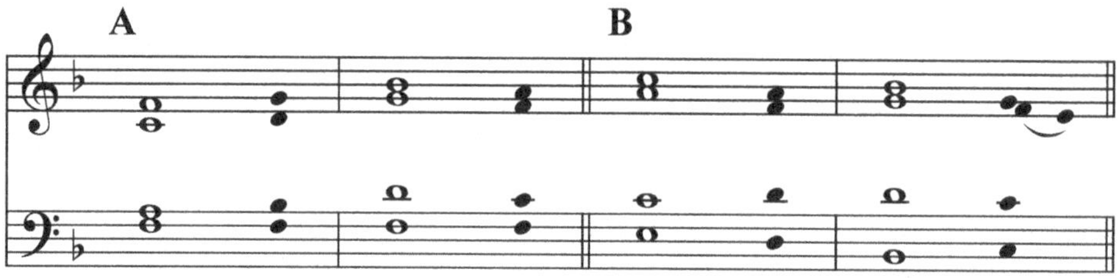

1 Come, let us sing to the LORD; *
let us shout for joy to the Rock of our salvation.
2 Let us come before his presence with thanksgiving *
and raise a loud shout to him with psalms. [ANT.]

3 For the LORD is a great God, *
and a great King above all gods.
4 In his hand are the caverns of the earth, *
and the heights of the hills are his also.
5 The sea is his, for he made it, *
and his hands have molded the dry land. [ANT.]

6 Come, let us bow down, and bend the knee, *
and kneel before the LORD our Maker.
7 For he is our God,
and we are the people of his pasture and the sheep of his hand. *
Oh, that today you would hearken to his voice! [ANT.]

A 8 Harden not your hearts,
as your forebears did in the wilderness, *
at Meribah, and on that day at Massah,
when they tempted me.
B 9 They put me to the test, *
though they had seen my works.
A 10 Forty years long I detested that generation and said, *
"This people are wayward in their hearts;
they do not know my ways."
B 11 So I swore in my wrath, *
"They shall not enter into my rest." [ANT.]

RCL Lent 4A   Psalm 23

based on "St. Columba" (H82–645)

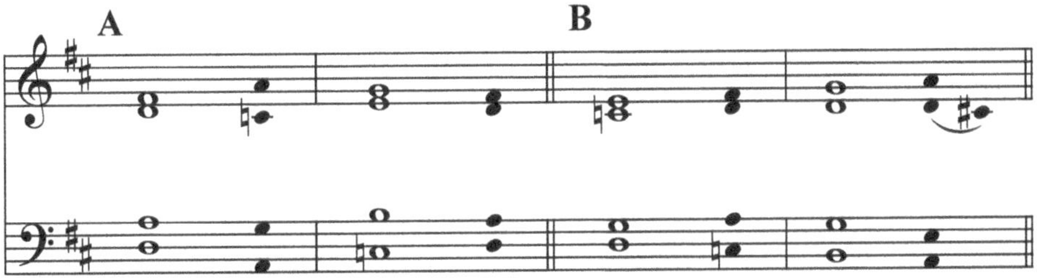

1 The LORD is my shepherd; *
    I shall not be in want.
2 He makes me lie down in green pastures *
    and leads me beside still waters. [ANT.]

3 He revives my soul *
    and guides me along right pathways for his Name's sake.
4 Though I walk through the valley of the shadow of death,
  I shall fear no evil; *
    for you are with me;
    your rod and your staff, they comfort me. [ANT.]

5 You spread a table before me in the presence of those
        who trouble me; *
    you have anointed my head with oil,
    and my cup is running over.
6 Surely your goodness and mercy shall follow me all the days
        of my life, *
    and I will dwell in the house of the LORD for ever. [ANT.]

RCL Lent 5A Psalm 130

based on "Pange lingua" (H82–166)

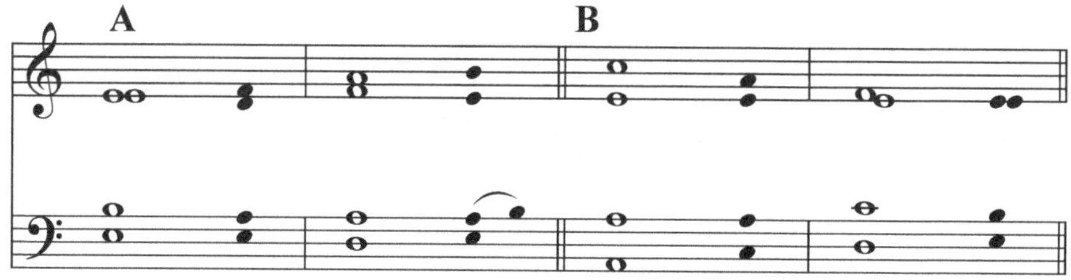

A 1 Out of the depths have I called to you, O LORD;
LORD, hear my voice; *
let your ears consider well the voice of my supplication.
A 2 If you, LORD, were to note what is done amiss, *
O LORD, who could stand?
B 3 For there is forgiveness with you; *
therefore you shall be feared. [ANT.]

4 I wait for the LORD; my soul waits for him; *
in his word is my hope.
5 My soul waits for the LORD,
more than watchmen for the morning, *
more than watchmen for the morning. [ANT.]

6 O Israel, wait for the LORD, *
for with the LORD there is mercy;
7 With him there is plenteous redemption, *
and he shall redeem Israel from all their sins. [ANT.]

For
Palm Sunday
through
Easter Week
see
Pages 110 – 141

RCL Easter 2A Psalm 16

based on "Rouen" (H82–360)

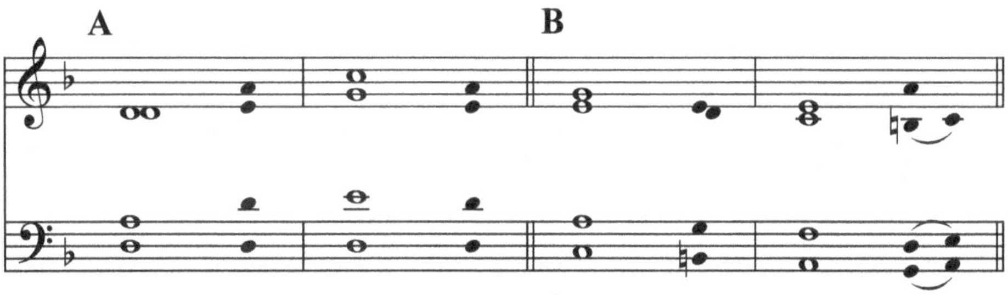

1 Protect me, O God, for I take refuge in you; *
I have said to the LORD, "You are my Lord,
my good above all other."
2 All my delight is upon the godly that are in the land, *
upon those who are noble among the people. [ANT.]

3 But those who run after other gods *
shall have their troubles multiplied.
4 Their libations of blood I will not offer, *
nor take the names of their gods upon my lips. [ANT.]

5 O LORD, you are my portion and my cup; *
it is you who uphold my lot.
6 My boundaries enclose a pleasant land; *
indeed, I have a goodly heritage. [ANT.]

7 I will bless the LORD who gives me counsel; *
my heart teaches me, night after night.
8 I have set the LORD always before me; *
because he is at my right hand I shall not fall. [ANT.]

A 9 My heart, therefore, is glad, and my spirit rejoices; *
my body also shall rest in hope.
A 10 For you will not abandon me to the grave, *
nor let your holy one see the Pit.
B 11 You will show me the path of life; *
in your presence there is fullness of joy,
and in your right hand are pleasures for evermore. [ANT.]

RCL Easter 3A Psalm 116: 1–3, 10–17

based on "Middlebury" (H82–213)

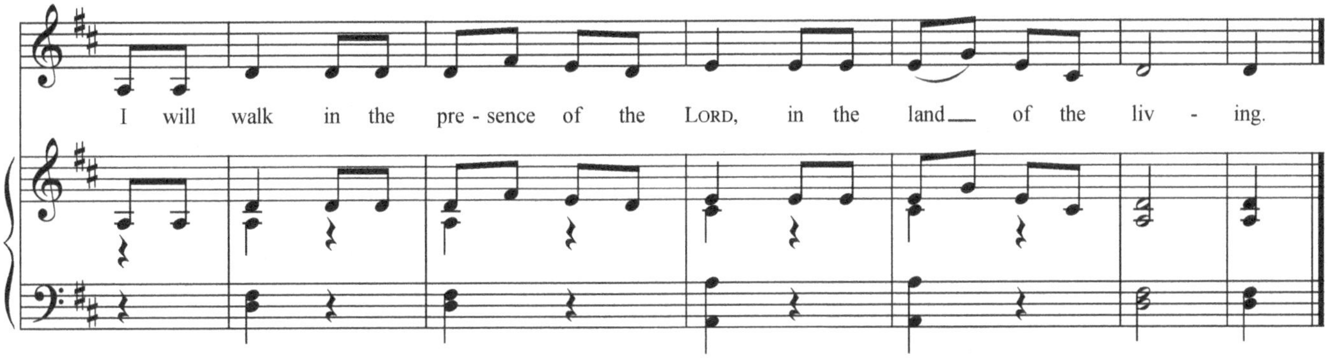

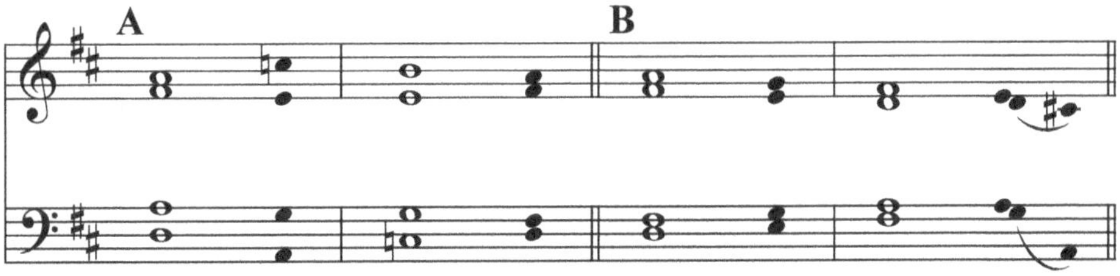

1 I love the LORD,
because he has heard the voice of my supplication, *
because he has inclined his ear to me
whenever I called upon him. [ANT.]

2 The cords of death entangled me;
the grip of the grave took hold of me; *
I came to grief and sorrow.
3 Then I called upon the Name of the LORD: *
"O LORD, I pray you, save my life." [ANT.]

A 10 How shall I repay the LORD *
for all the good things he has done for me?
A 11 I will lift up the cup of salvation *
and call upon the Name of the LORD.
B 12 I will fulfill my vows to the LORD *
in the presence of all his people. [ANT.]

13 Precious in the sight of the LORD *
is the death of his servants.
14 O LORD, I am your servant; *
I am your servant and the child of your handmaid;
you have freed me from my bonds. [ANT.]

A 15 I will offer you the sacrifice of thanksgiving *
and call upon the Name of the LORD.
A 16 I will fulfill my vows to the LORD *
in the presence of all his people,
B 17 In the courts of the LORD's house, *
in the midst of you, O Jerusalem.
Hallelujah! [ANT.]

RCL Easter 4A   Psalm 23

based on "St. Columba" (H82–645)

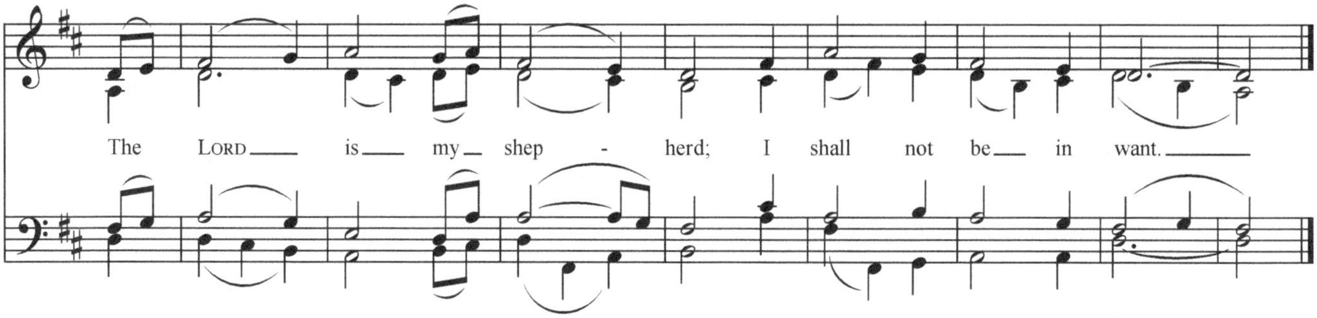

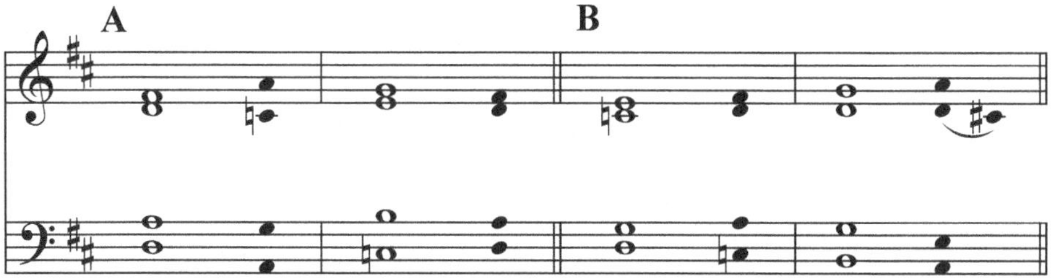

1 The LORD is my shepherd; *
I shall not be in want.
2 He makes me lie down in green pastures *
and leads me beside still waters. [ANT.]

3 He revives my soul *
and guides me along right pathways for his Name's sake.
4 Though I walk through the valley of the shadow of death,
I shall fear no evil; *
for you are with me;
your rod and your staff, they comfort me. [ANT.]

5 You spread a table before me in the presence of those
who trouble me; *
you have anointed my head with oil,
and my cup is running over.
6 Surely your goodness and mercy shall follow me all the days
of my life, *
and I will dwell in the house of the LORD for ever. [ANT.]

RCL Easter 5A   Psalm 31: 1–5, 15–16

based on "Christe sanctorum" (H82–1)

1 In you, O LORD, have I taken refuge;
let me never be put to shame: *
deliver me in your righteousness.
2 Incline your ear to me; *
make haste to deliver me. [ANT.]

3 Be my strong rock, a castle to keep me safe,
for you are my crag and my stronghold; *
for the sake of your Name, lead me and guide me.
4 Take me out of the net that they have secretly set for me, *
for you are my tower of strength. [ANT.]

A 5 Into your hands I commend my spirit, *
for you have redeemed me,
O LORD, O God of truth.
B 15 My times are in your hand; *
rescue me from the hand of my enemies,
and from those who persecute me.
B 16 Make your face to shine upon your servant, *
and in your loving-kindness save me." [ANT.]

RCL Easter 6A **Psalm 66: 7–18**

based on "Moscow" (H82–537)

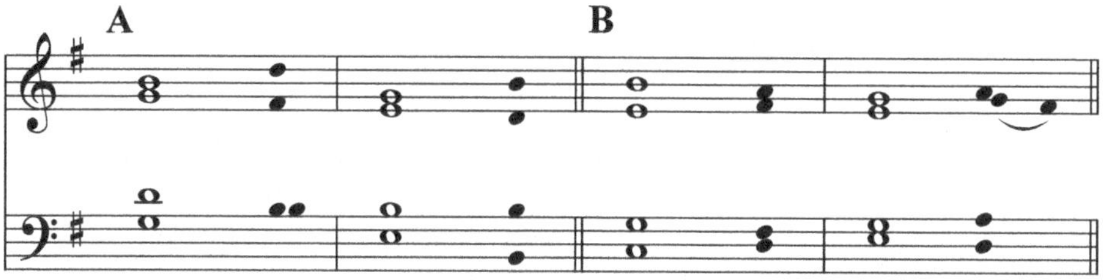

7 Bless our God, you peoples; *
make the voice of his praise to be heard;
8 Who holds our souls in life, *
and will not allow our feet to slip. [ANT.]

A 9 For you, O God, have proved us; *
you have tried us just as silver is tried.
A 10 You brought us into the snare; *
you laid heavy burdens upon our backs.
B 11 You let enemies ride over our heads;
we went through fire and water; *
but you brought us out into a place of refreshment. [ANT.]

12 I will enter your house with burnt-offerings
and will pay you my vows, *
which I promised with my lips
and spoke with my mouth when I was in trouble.
13 I will offer you sacrifices of fat beasts
with the smoke of rams; *
I will give you oxen and goats. [ANT.]

14 Come and listen, all you who fear God, *
and I will tell you what he has done for me.
15 I called out to him with my mouth, *
and his praise was on my tongue.

A 16 If I had found evil in my heart, *
the LORD would not have heard me;
A 17 But in truth God has heard me; *
he has attended to the voice of my prayer.
B 18 Blessed be God, who has not rejected my prayer, *
nor withheld his love from me. [ANT.]

For
Ascension Day
see
Pages 142 – 143

RCL Easter 7A   Psalm 68: 1–10, 33–36

based on "Hyfrydol" (H82–460)

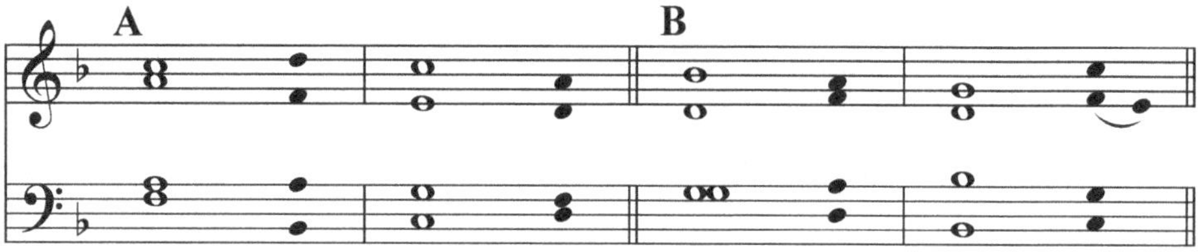

A 1 Let God arise, and let his enemies be scattered; *
let those who hate him flee before him.
A 2 Let them vanish like smoke when the wind drives it away; *
as the wax melts at the fire, so let the wicked perish at
the presence of God.
B 3 But let the righteous be glad and rejoice before God; *
let them also be merry and joyful. [ANT.]

A 4 Sing to God, sing praises to his Name;
exalt him who rides upon the heavens; *
YAHWEH is his Name, rejoice before him!
A 5 Father of orphans, defender of widows, *
God in his holy habitation!
B 6 God gives the solitary a home and brings forth prisoners
into freedom; *
but the rebels shall live in dry places. [ANT.]

7 O God, when you went forth before your people, *
when you marched through the wilderness,
8 The earth shook, and the skies poured down rain,
at the presence of God, the God of Sinai, *
at the presence of God, the God of Israel. [ANT.]

9 You sent a gracious rain, O God, upon your inheritance; *
you refreshed the land when it was weary.
10 Your people found their home in it; *
in your goodness, O God, you have made provision
for the poor. [ANT.]

A 34 He rides in the heavens, the ancient heavens; *
he sends forth his voice, his mighty voice.
A 35 Ascribe power to God; *
his majesty is over Israel;
his strength is in the skies.
B 36 How wonderful is God in his holy places! *
the God of Israel giving strength and power to his people!
Blessed be God! [ANT.]

For
Pentecost
see
Pages 144 – 149

Year B

RCL Advent 1B Psalm 80: 1–7, 16–18

based on "Nun komm, der Heiden Heiland" (H82–54)

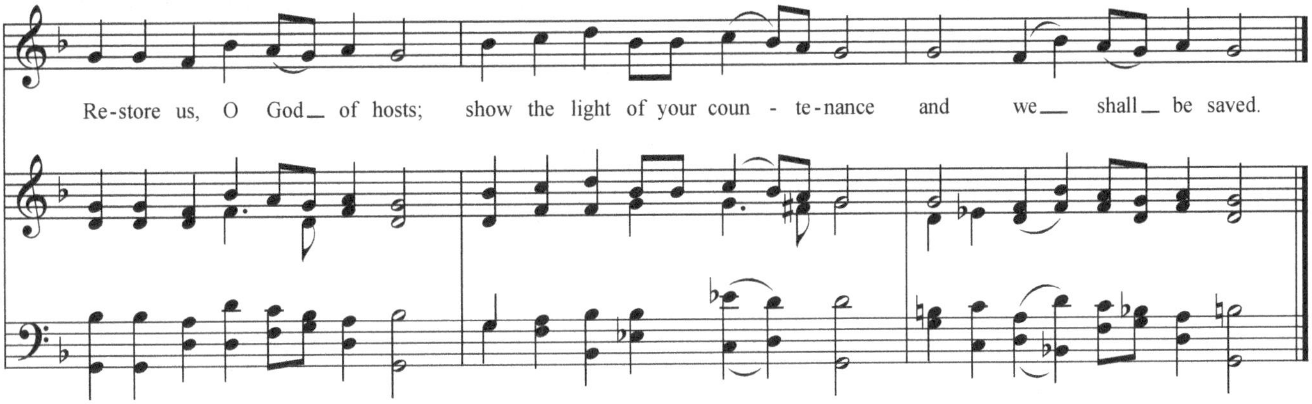

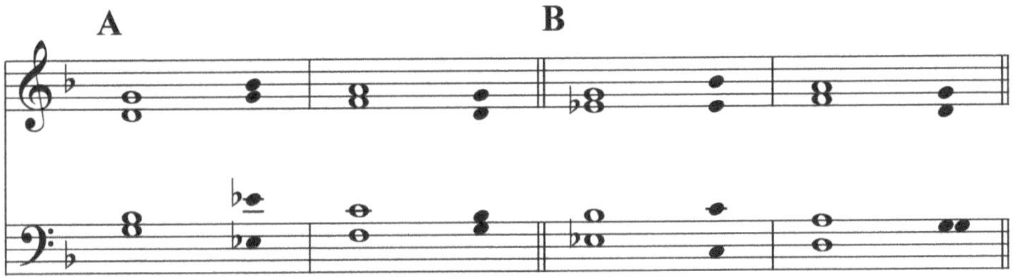

1 Hear, O Shepherd of Israel, leading Joseph like a flock; *
  shine forth, you that are enthroned upon the cherubim.
2 In the presence of Ephraim, Benjamin, and Manasseh, *
  stir up your strength and come to help us. [ANT.]

A 4 O Lord God of hosts, *
  how long will you be angered
  despite the prayers of your people?
A 5 You have fed them with the bread of tears; *
  you have given them bowls of tears to drink.
B 6 You have made us the derision of our neighbors, *
  and our enemies laugh us to scorn. [ANT.]

16 Let your hand be upon the man of your right hand, *
  the son of man you have made so strong for yourself.
17 And so will we never turn away from you; *
  give us life, that we may call upon your Name. [ANT.]

RCL Advent 2B Psalm 85: 1–2, 8–13

based on "Conditor alme siderum" (H82–60)

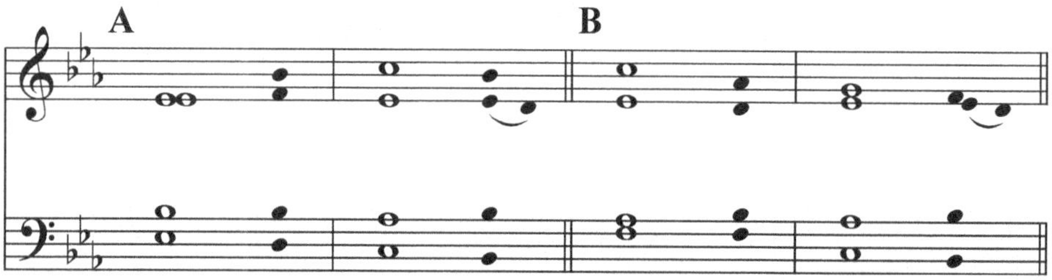

1 You have been gracious to your land, O LORD, *
you have restored the good fortune of Jacob.
2 You have forgiven the iniquity of your people *
and blotted out all their sins. [ANT.]

8 I will listen to what the LORD God is saying, *
for he is speaking peace to his faithful people
and to those who turn their hearts to him.
9 Truly, his salvation is very near to those who fear him, *
that his glory may dwell in our land. [ANT.]

10 Mercy and truth have met together; *
righteousness and peace have kissed each other.
11 Truth shall spring up from the earth, *
and righteousness shall look down from heaven. [ANT.]

12 The LORD will indeed grant prosperity, *
and our land will yield its increase.
13 Righteousness shall go before him, *
and peace shall be a pathway for his feet. [ANT.]

RCL Advent 3B Psalm 126

based on "St. Stephen" (H82–73)

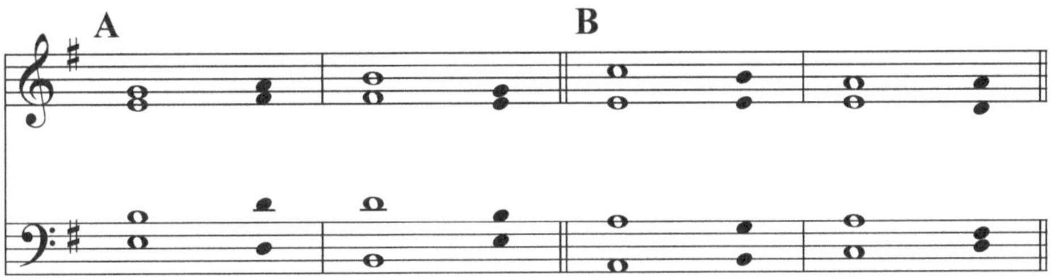

A 1 When the Lord restored the fortunes of Zion, *
then were we like those who dream.
A 2 Then was our mouth filled with laughter, *
and our tongue with shouts of joy.
B 3 Then they said among the nations, *
"The Lord has done great things for them." [ANT.]

A 5 Restore our fortunes, O Lord, *
like the watercourses of the Negev.
A 6 Those who sowed with tears *
will reap with songs of joy.
B 7 Those who go out weeping, carrying the seed, *
will come again with joy, shouldering their sheaves. [ANT.]

RCL Advent 3B Canticle 15

based on "Birmingham" (H82–437)

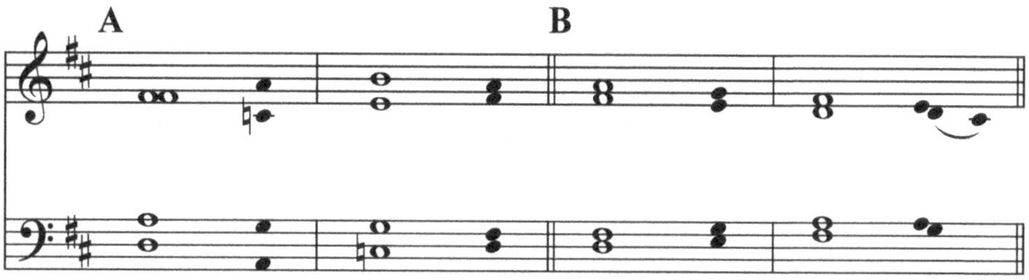

1 My soul proclaims the greatness of the Lord,
my spirit rejoices in God my Savior, *
for he has looked with favor on his lowly servant.
2 From this day all generations will call me blessed: *
the Almighty has done great things for me,
and holy is his Name. [ANT.]

3 He has mercy on those who fear him *
in every generation.
4 He has shown the strength of his arm,
he has scattered the proud in their conceit. [ANT.]

5 He has cast down the mighty from their thrones, *
and has lifted up the lowly.
6 He has filled the hungry with good things, *
and the rich he has sent away empty. [ANT.]

7 He has come to the help of his servant Israel, *
for he has remembered his promise of mercy,
8 The promise he has made to our fathers, *
to Abraham and his children for ever. [ANT.]

RCL Advent 4B Canticle 15

based on "Birmingham" (H82–437)

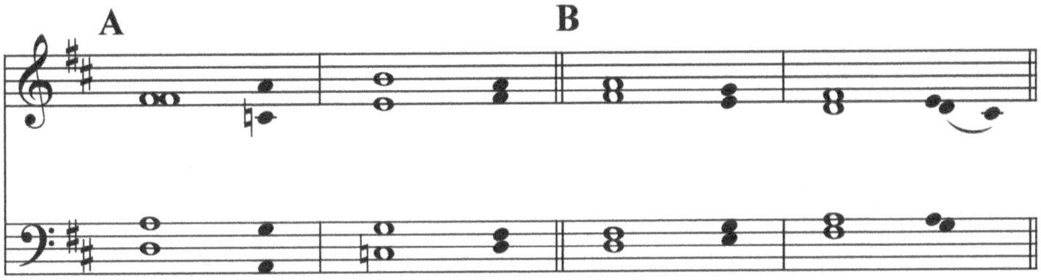

1 My soul proclaims the greatness of the Lord,
my spirit rejoices in God my Savior, *
for he has looked with favor on his lowly servant.
2 From this day all generations will call me blessed: *
the Almighty has done great things for me,
and holy is his Name. [ANT.]

3 He has mercy on those who fear him *
in every generation.
4 He has shown the strength of his arm,
he has scattered the proud in their conceit. [ANT.]

5 He has cast down the mighty from their thrones, *
and has lifted up the lowly.
6 He has filled the hungry with good things, *
and the rich he has sent away empty. [ANT.]

7 He has come to the help of his servant Israel, *
for he has remembered his promise of mercy,
8 The promise he has made to our fathers, *
to Abraham and his children for ever. [ANT.]

RCL Advent 4B **Psalm 89: 1–4, 19–26**

based on "Eventide" (H82–662)

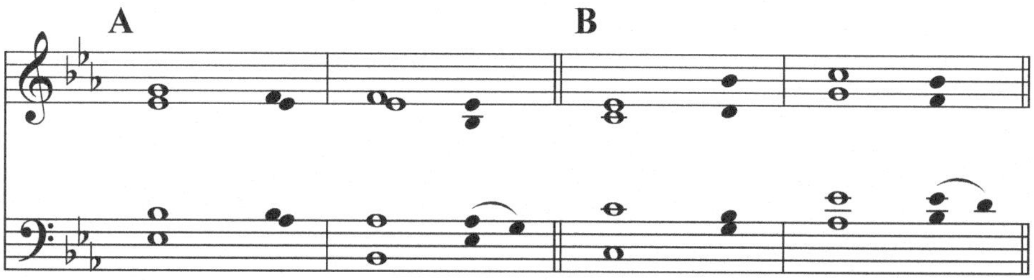

1 Your love, O LORD, for ever will I sing; *
from age to age my mouth will proclaim your faithfulness.
2 For I am persuaded that your love is established for ever; *
you have set your faithfulness firmly in the heavens. [ANT.]

3 "I have made a covenant with my chosen one; *
I have sworn an oath to David my servant:
4 'I will establish your line for ever, *
and preserve your throne for all generations.'" [ANT.]

19 You spoke once in a vision and said to your faithful people: *
"I have set the crown upon a warrior
and have exalted one chosen out of the people.
20 I have found David my servant; *
with my holy oil have I anointed him. [ANT.]

A 21 My hand will hold him fast *
and my arm will make him strong.
B 22 No enemy shall deceive him, *
nor any wicked man bring him down.
A 23 I will crush his foes before him *
and strike down those who hate him.
B 24 My faithfulness and love shall be with him, *
and he shall be victorious through my Name. [ANT.]

25 I shall make his dominion extend *
from the Great Sea to the River.
26 He will say to me, 'You are my Father, *
my God, and the rock of my salvation.'" [ANT.]

For
Christmas
through
Epiphany 1
see
Pages 98–105

RCL Epiphany 2B Psalm 139: 1–5, 12–17

based on "Tender Thought" (H82–702)

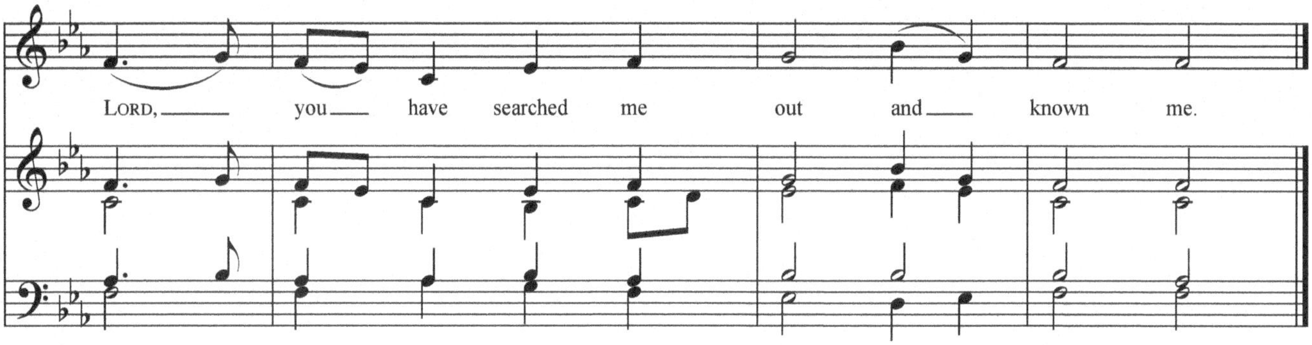

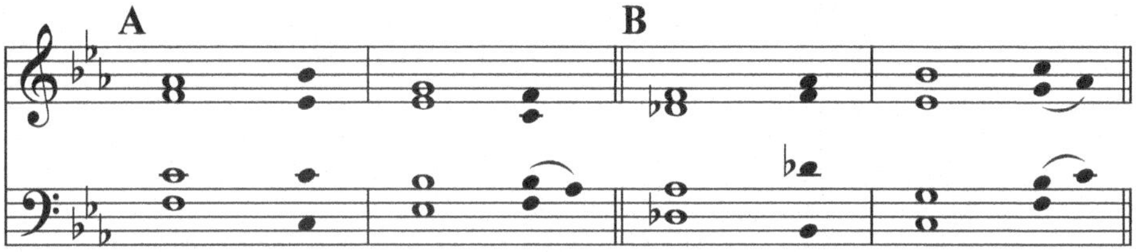

1 LORD, you have searched me out and known me; *
you know my sitting down and my rising up;
you discern my thoughts from afar.
2 You trace my journeys and my resting-places *
and are acquainted with all my ways. [ANT.]

A 3 Indeed, there is not a word on my lips, *
but you, O LORD, know it altogether.
A 4 You press upon me behind and before *
and lay your hand upon me.
B 5 Such knowledge is too wonderful for me; *
it is so high that I cannot attain to it. [ANT.]

12 For you yourself created my inmost parts; *
you knit me together in my mother's womb.
13 I will thank you because I am marvelously made; *
your works are wonderful, and I know it well. [ANT.]

A 14 My body was not hidden from you, *
while I was being made in secret
and woven in the depths of the earth.
A 15 Your eyes beheld my limbs, yet unfinished in the womb;
all of them were written in your book; *
B they were fashioned day by day,
when as yet there was none of them. [ANT.]

16 How deep I find your thoughts, O God! *
how great is the sum of them!
17 If I were to count them,
they would be more in number than the sand; *
to count them all,
my life span would need to be like yours. [ANT.]

RCL Epiphany 3B **Psalm 62: 6–14**

based on "Eventide" (H82–662)

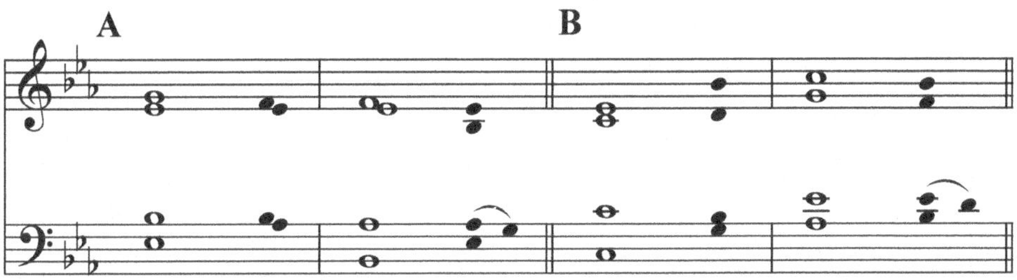

6 For God alone my soul in silence waits; *
truly, my hope is in him.
7 He alone is my rock and my salvation, *
my stronghold, so that I shall not be shaken. [ANT.]

8 In God is my safety and my honor; *
God is my strong rock and my refuge.
9 Put your trust in him always, O people, *
pour out your hearts before him, for God is our refuge. [ANT.]

10 Those of high degree are but a fleeting breath, *
even those of low estate cannot be trusted.
11 On the scales they are lighter than a breath, *
all of them together. [ANT.]

A 12 Put no trust in extortion;
in robbery take no empty pride; *
though wealth increase, set not your heart upon it.
A 13 God has spoken once, twice have I heard it, *
that power belongs to God.
B 14 Steadfast love is yours, O Lord, *
for you repay everyone according to his deeds. [ANT.]

RCL Epiphany 4B Psalm 111

based on "Picardy" (H82–324)

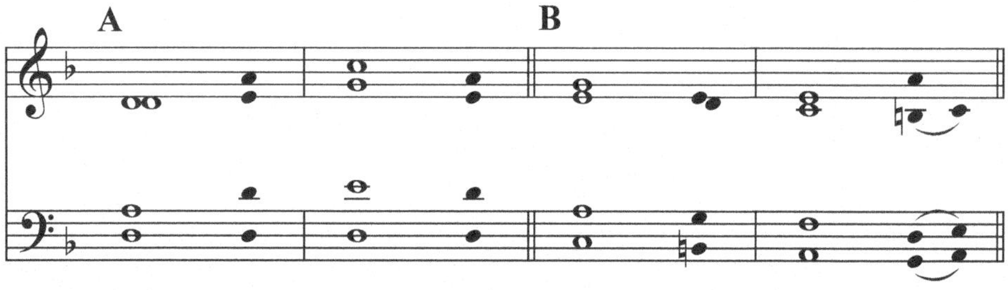

1 Hallelujah!
I will give thanks to the LORD with my whole heart, *
in the assembly of the upright, in the congregation.
2 Great are the deeds of the LORD! *
they are studied by all who delight in them. [ANT.]

3 His work is full of majesty and splendor, *
and his righteousness endures for ever.
4 He makes his marvelous works to be remembered; *
the LORD is gracious and full of compassion. [ANT.]

5 He gives food to those who fear him; *
he is ever mindful of his covenant.
6 He has shown his people the power of his works *
in giving them the lands of the nations. [ANT.]

7 The works of his hands are faithfulness and justice; *
all his commandments are sure.
8 They stand fast for ever and ever, *
because they are done in truth and equity. [ANT.]

9 He sent redemption to his people;
he commanded his covenant for ever; *
holy and awesome is his Name.
10 The fear of the LORD is the beginning of wisdom; *
those who act accordingly have a good understanding;
his praise endures for ever. [ANT.]

For
The Presentation, February 2
see
Page 106 – 107

RCL Epiphany 5B **Psalm 147: 1–12, 21c**

based on "Birmingham" (H82–437)

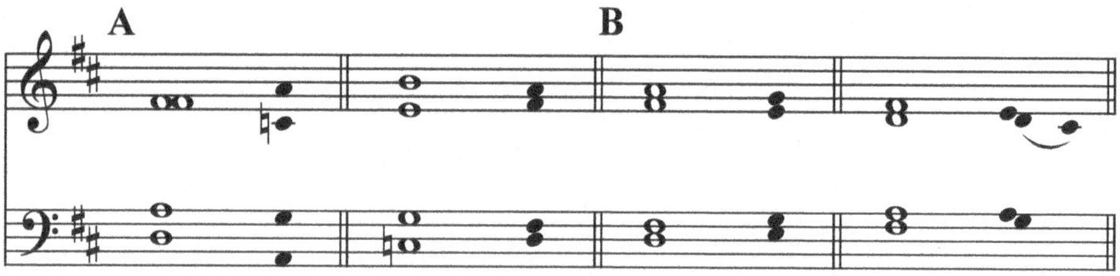

A 1 Hallelujah!
How good it is to sing praises to our God! *
how pleasant it is to honor him with praise!
A 2 The LORD rebuilds Jerusalem; *
he gathers the exiles of Israel.
B 3 He heals the brokenhearted *
and binds up their wounds. [ANT.]

4 He counts the number of the stars *
and calls them all by their names.
5 Great is our LORD and mighty in power; *
there is no limit to his wisdom. [ANT.]

6 The LORD lifts up the lowly, *
but casts the wicked to the ground.
7 Sing to the LORD with thanksgiving; *
make music to our God upon the harp. [ANT.]

A 8 He covers the heavens with clouds *
and prepares rain for the earth;
A 9 He makes grass to grow upon the mountains *
and green plants to serve mankind.
B 10 He provides food for flocks and herds *
and for the young ravens when they cry. [ANT.]

11 He is not impressed by the might of a horse; *
he has no pleasure in the strength of a man;
12/21c But the LORD has pleasure in those who fear him, *
in those who await his gracious favor.
Hallelujah! [ANT.]

RCL Epiphany 6B **Psalm 30**

based on "Wer nur den lieben Gott" (H82–635)

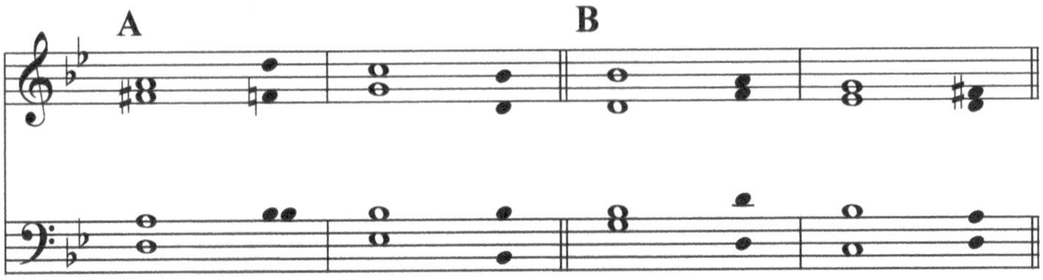

A 1 I will exalt you, O LORD,
because you have lifted me up *
and have not let my enemies triumph over me.
A 2 O LORD my God, I cried out to you, *
and you restored me to health.
B 3 You brought me up, O LORD, from the dead; *
you restored my life as I was going down to the grave. [ANT.]

A 4 Sing to the LORD, you servants of his; *
give thanks for the remembrance of his holiness.
A 5 For his wrath endures but the twinkling of an eye, *
his favor for a lifetime.
B 6 Weeping may spend the night, *
but joy comes in the morning. [ANT.]

7 While I felt secure, I said,
"I shall never be disturbed. *
You, LORD, with your favor, made me as strong as
the mountains."
8 Then you hid your face, *
and I was filled with fear. [ANT.]

A 9 I cried to you, O LORD; *
I pleaded with the LORD, saying,
A 10 "What profit is there in my blood, if I go down to the Pit? *
will the dust praise you or declare your faithfulness?
B 11 Hear, O LORD, and have mercy upon me; *
O LORD, be my helper." [ANT.]

12 You have turned my wailing into dancing; *
you have put off my sack-cloth and clothed me with joy.
13 Therefore my heart sings to you without ceasing; *
O LORD my God, I will give you thanks for ever. [ANT.]

RCL Epiphany 7B Psalm 41

based on "St. Ethelwald" (H82–628)

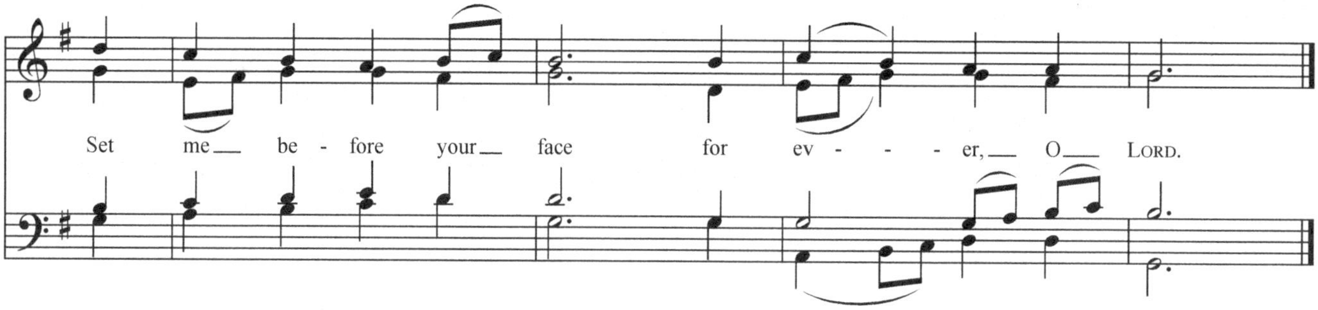

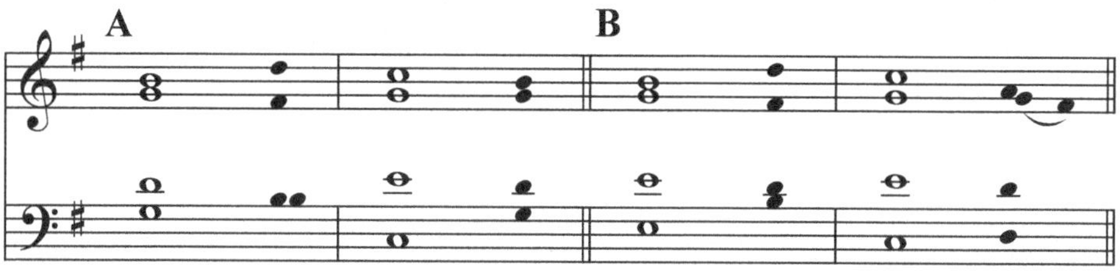

A 1 Happy are they who consider the poor and needy! *
the LORD will deliver them in the time of trouble.
A 2 The LORD preserves them and keeps them alive,
so that they may be happy in the land; *
he does not hand them over to the will of their enemies.
B 3 The LORD sustains them on their sickbed *
and ministers to them in their illness. [ANT.]

A 4 I said, "LORD, be merciful to me; *
heal me, for I have sinned against you."
A 5 My enemies are saying wicked things about me: *
"When will he die, and his name perish?"
B 6 Even if they come to see me, they speak empty words; *
their heart collects false rumors;
they go outside and spread them. [ANT.]

A 7 All my enemies whisper together about me *
and devise evil against me.
A 8 "A deadly thing," they say, "has fastened on him; *
he has taken to his bed and will never get up again."
B 9 Even my best friend, whom I trusted,
who broke bread with me, *
has lifted up his heel and turned against me. [ANT.]

A 10 But you, O LORD, be merciful to me and raise me up, *
and I shall repay them.
B 11 By this I know you are pleased with me, *
that my enemy does not triumph over me.
A 12 In my integrity you hold me fast, *
and shall set me before your face for ever.
B 13 Blessed be the LORD God of Israel, *
from age to age. Amen. Amen. [ANT.]

RCL Epiphany 8B   Psalm 103: 1–13, 22

based on "Wondrous Love" (H82–439)

1 Bless the LORD, O my soul, *
and all that is within me, bless his holy Name.
2 Bless the LORD, O my soul, *
and forget not all his benefits. [ANT.]

3 He forgives all your sins *
and heals all your infirmities;
4 He redeems your life from the grave *
and crowns you with mercy and loving-kindness; [ANT.]

A 5 He satisfies you with good things, *
and your youth is renewed like an eagle's.
A 6 The LORD executes righteousness *
and judgment for all who are oppressed.
B 7 He made his ways known to Moses *
and his works to the children of Israel. [ANT.]

A 9 He will not always accuse us, *
nor will he keep his anger for ever.
B 10 He has not dealt with us according to our sins, *
nor rewarded us according to our wickedness.
A 11 For as the heavens are high above the earth, *
so is his mercy great upon those who fear him.
B 12 As far as the east is from the west, *
so far has he removed our sins from us. [ANT.]

13 As a father cares for his children, *
so does the LORD care for those who fear him.
22 Bless the LORD, all you works of his,
in all places of his dominion; *
bless the LORD, O my soul. [ANT.]

RCL Epiphany Last Psalm 50: 1–6

based on "Leoni" (H82–401)

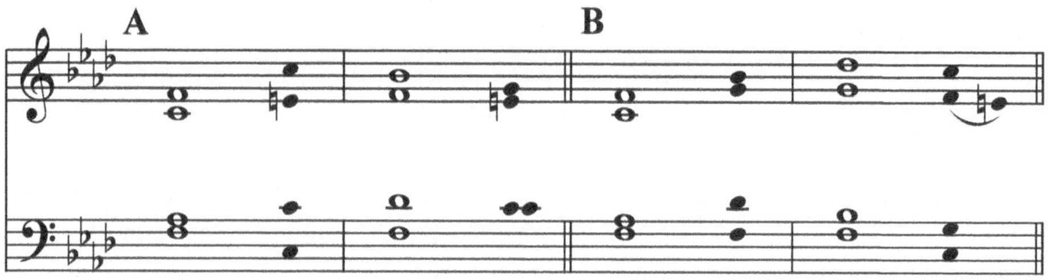

A 1 The LORD, the God of gods, has spoken; *
he has called the earth from the rising of the sun to
its setting.
A 2 Out of Zion, perfect in its beauty, *
God reveals himself in glory.
B 3 Our God will come and will not keep silence; *
before him there is a consuming flame,
and round about him a raging storm. [ANT.]

A 4 He calls the heavens and the earth from above *
to witness the judgment of his people.
A 5 "Gather before me my loyal followers, *
those who have made a covenant with me
and sealed it with sacrifice."
B 6 Let the heavens declare the rightness of his cause; *
for God himself is judge. [ANT.]

For
Ash Wednesday
see
Page 108

RCL Lent 1B   Psalm 25: 1–9

based on "Song 1" (H82–499)

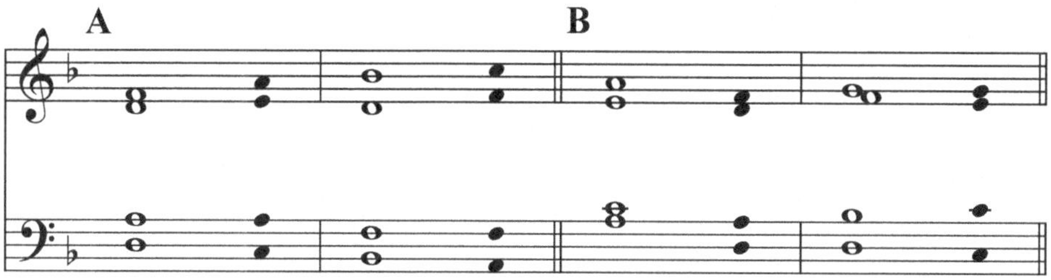

A 1 To you, O LORD, I lift up my soul;
my God, I put my trust in you; *
A let me not be humiliated,
nor let my enemies triumph over me.
B 2 Let none who look to you be put to shame; *
let the treacherous be disappointed in their schemes. [ANT.]

3 Show me your ways, O LORD, *
and teach me your paths.
4 Lead me in your truth and teach me, *
for you are the God of my salvation;
in you have I trusted all the day long. [ANT.]

5 Remember, O LORD, your compassion and love, *
for they are from everlasting.
6 Remember not the sins of my youth and my transgressions; *
remember me according to your love
and for the sake of your goodness, O LORD. [ANT.]

A 7 Gracious and upright is the LORD; *
therefore he teaches sinners in his way.
A 8 He guides the humble in doing right *
and teaches his way to the lowly.
B 9 All the paths of the LORD are love and faithfulness *
to those who keep his covenant and his testimonies. [ANT.]

RCL Lent 2B Psalm 22: 22–30

based on "Charlestown" (H82–571)

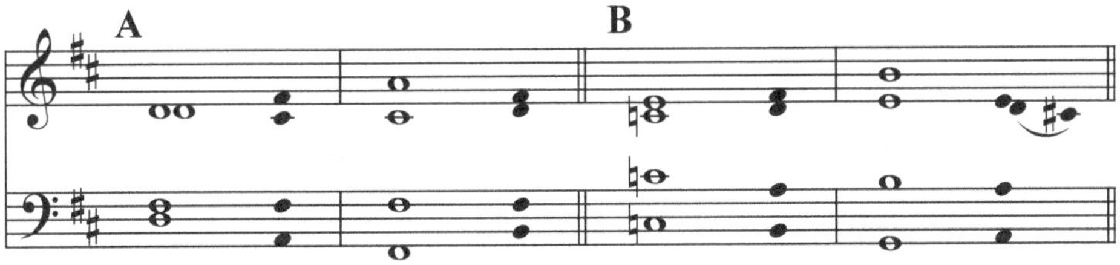

22 Praise the LORD, you that fear him; *
stand in awe of him, O offspring of Israel;
all you of Jacob's line, give glory.
23 For he does not despise nor abhor the poor in their poverty;
neither does he hide his face from them; *
but when they cry to him he hears them. [ANT.]

24 My praise is of him in the great assembly; *
I will perform my vows in the presence of those who
worship him.
25 The poor shall eat and be satisfied,
and those who seek the LORD shall praise him: *
"May your heart live for ever!" [ANT.]

A 26 All the ends of the earth shall remember and turn to
the LORD, *
and all the families of the nations shall bow before him.
A 27 For kingship belongs to the LORD; *
he rules over the nations.
B 28 To him alone all who sleep in the earth bow down
in worship; *
all who go down to the dust fall before him. [ANT.]

29 My soul shall live for him;
my descendants shall serve him; *
they shall be known as the LORD's for ever.
30 They shall come and make known to a people yet unborn *
the saving deeds that he has done. [ANT.]

RCL Lent 3B Psalm 19

based on "Song 1" (H82–499)

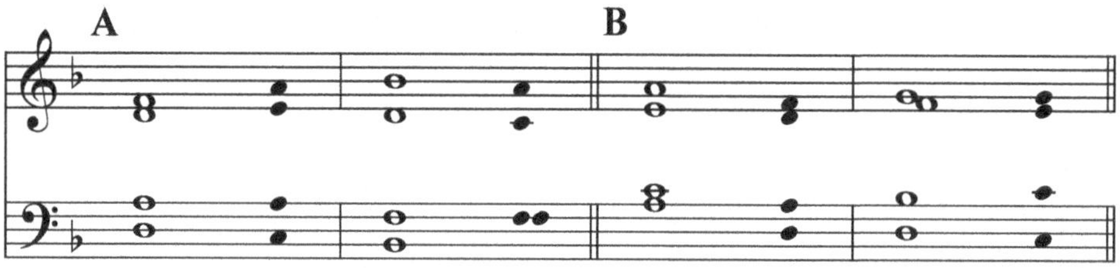

A 1 The heavens declare the glory of God, *
and the firmament shows his handiwork.
B 2 One day tells its tale to another, *
and one night imparts knowledge to another.
A 3 Although they have no words or language, *
and their voices are not heard,
B 4 Their sound has gone out into all lands, *
and their message to the ends of the world. [ANT.]

5 In the deep has he set a pavilion for the sun; *
it comes forth like a bridegroom out of his chamber;
it rejoices like a champion to run its course.
6 It goes forth from the uttermost edge of the heavens
and runs about to the end of it again; *
nothing is hidden from its burning heat. [ANT.]

7 The law of the LORD is perfect
and revives the soul; *
the testimony of the LORD is sure
and gives wisdom to the innocent.
8 The statutes of the LORD are just
and rejoice the heart; *
the commandment of the LORD is clear
and gives light to the eyes. [ANT.]

9 The fear of the LORD is clean
and endures for ever; *
the judgments of the LORD are true
and righteous altogether.
10 More to be desired are they than gold,
more than much fine gold, *
sweeter far than honey,
than honey in the comb. [ANT.]

11 By them also is your servant enlightened, *
and in keeping them there is great reward.
12 Who can tell how often he offends? *
cleanse me from my secret faults. [ANT.]

13 Above all, keep your servant from presumptuous sins;
let them not get dominion over me; *
then shall I be whole and sound,
and innocent of a great offense.
14 Let the words of my mouth and the meditation of my
heart be acceptable in your sight, *
O LORD, my strength and my redeemer. [ANT.]

RCL Lent 4B Psalm 107: 1–3, 17–22

based on "Darwall's 148th" (H82–625)

A 1 Give thanks to the LORD, for he is good, *
and his mercy endures for ever.
A 2 Let all those whom the LORD has redeemed proclaim *
that he redeemed them from the hand of the foe.
B 3 He gathered them out of the lands; *
from the east and from the west,
from the north and from the south. [ANT.]

17 Some were fools and took to rebellious ways; *
they were afflicted because of their sins.
18 They abhorred all manner of food *
and drew near to death's door. [ANT.]

19 Then they cried to the LORD in their trouble, *
and he delivered them from their distress.
20 He sent forth his word and healed them *
and saved them from the grave. [ANT.]

21 Let them give thanks to the LORD for his mercy *
and the wonders he does for his children.
22 Let them offer a sacrifice of thanksgiving *
and tell of his acts with shouts of joy. [ANT.]

RCL Lent 5B Psalm 51: 1–13

based on "Eventide" (H82–662)

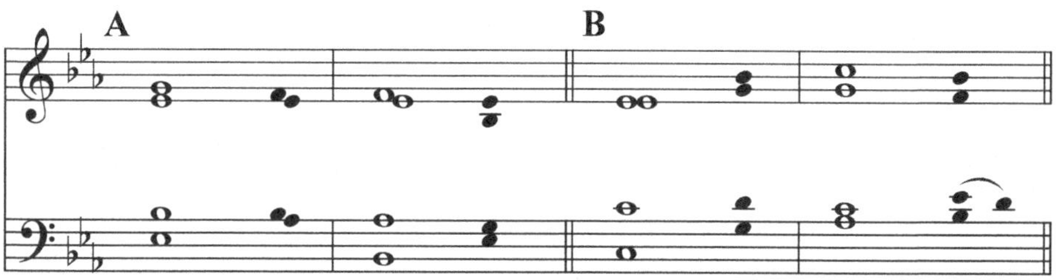

1 Have mercy on me, O God, according to your loving-kindness; *
in your great compassion blot out my offenses.
2 Wash me through and through from my wickedness *
and cleanse me from my sin. [ANT.]

A 3 For I know my transgressions, *
and my sin is ever before me.
A 4 Against you only have I sinned *
and done what is evil in your sight.
B 5 And so you are justified when you speak *
and upright in your judgment. [ANT.]

6 Indeed, I have been wicked from my birth, *
a sinner from my mother's womb.
7 For behold, you look for truth deep within me, *
and will make me understand wisdom secretly. [ANT.]

A 8 Purge me from my sin, and I shall be pure; *
wash me, and I shall be clean indeed.
A 9 Make me hear of joy and gladness, *
that the body you have broken may rejoice.
B 10 Hide your face from my sins *
and blot out all my iniquities. [ANT.]

A 11 Create in me a clean heart, O God, *
and renew a right spirit within me.
A 12 Cast me not away from your presence *
and take not your holy Spirit from me.
B 13 Give me the joy of your saving help again *
and sustain me with your bountiful Spirit. [ANT.]

RCL Lent 5B Psalm 119: 9–16

based on "Hymn to Joy" (H82–376)

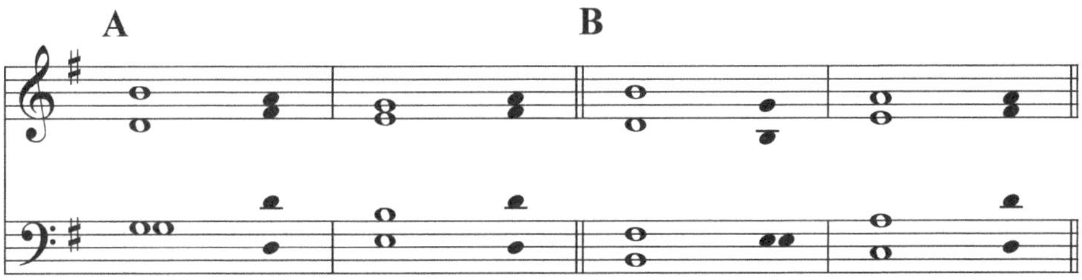

9 How shall a young man cleanse his way? *
By keeping to your words.
10 With my whole heart I seek you; *
let me not stray from your commandments. [ANT.]

11 I treasure your promise in my heart, *
that I may not sin against you.
12 Blessed are you, O LORD; *
instruct me in your statutes. [ANT.]

13 With my lips will I recite *
all the judgments of your mouth.
14 I have taken greater delight in the way of your decrees *
than in all manner of riches. [ANT.]

15 I will meditate on your commandments *
and give attention to your ways.
16 My delight is in your statutes; *
I will not forget your word. [ANT.]

For
Palm Sunday
through
Easter Week
see
Pages 110 – 141

RCL Easter 2B Psalm 133

based on "Ellacombe" (H82–210)

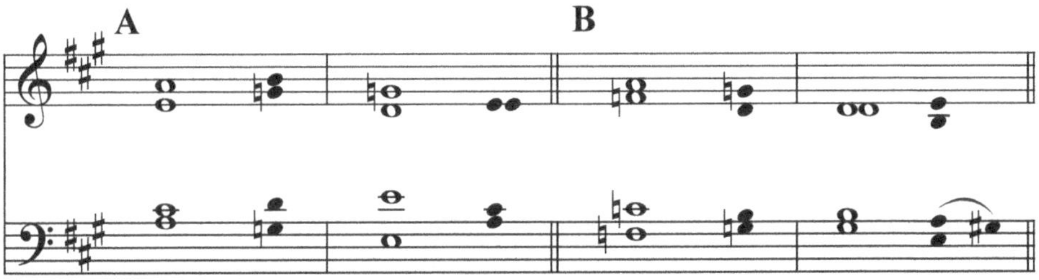

A 1 Oh, how good and pleasant it is, *
when brethren live together in unity!
A 2 It is like fine oil upon the head *
that runs down upon the beard,
B 3 Upon the beard of Aaron, *
and runs down upon the collar of his robe. [ANT.]

4 It is like the dew of Hermon *
that falls upon the hills of Zion.
5 For there the LORD has ordained the blessing: *
life for evermore. [ANT.]

RCL Easter 3B Psalm 4

based on "Noël nouvelet" (H82–204)

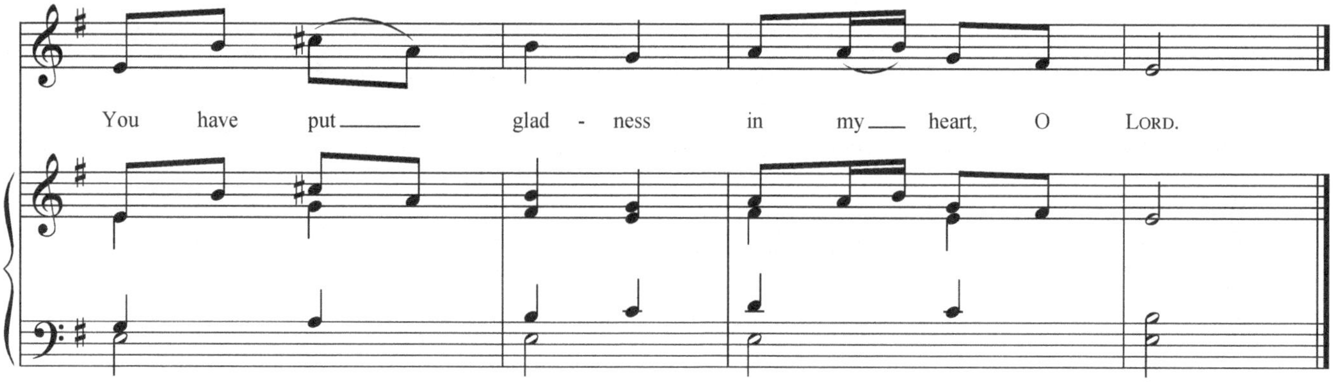

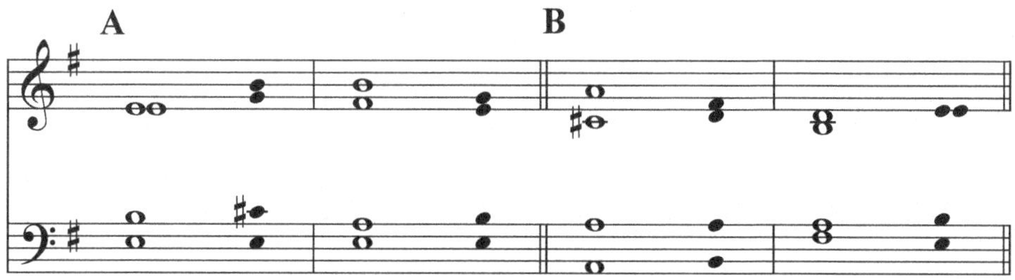

1 Answer me when I call, O God, defender of my cause; *
you set me free when I am hard-pressed;
have mercy on me and hear my prayer.
2 "You mortals, how long will you dishonor my glory? *
how long will you worship dumb idols
and run after false gods?" [ANT.]

A 3 Know that the LORD does wonders for the faithful; *
when I call upon the LORD, he will hear me.
A 4 Tremble, then, and do not sin; *
speak to your heart in silence upon your bed.
B 5 Offer the appointed sacrifices *
and put your trust in the LORD. [ANT.]

A 6 Many are saying,
"Oh, that we might see better times!" *
Lift up the light of your countenance upon us, O LORD.
A 7 You have put gladness in my heart, *
more than when grain and wine and oil increase.
B 8 I lie down in peace; at once I fall asleep; *
for only you, LORD, make me dwell in safety. [ANT.]

RCL Easter 4B Psalm 23

based on "St. Columba" (H82–645)

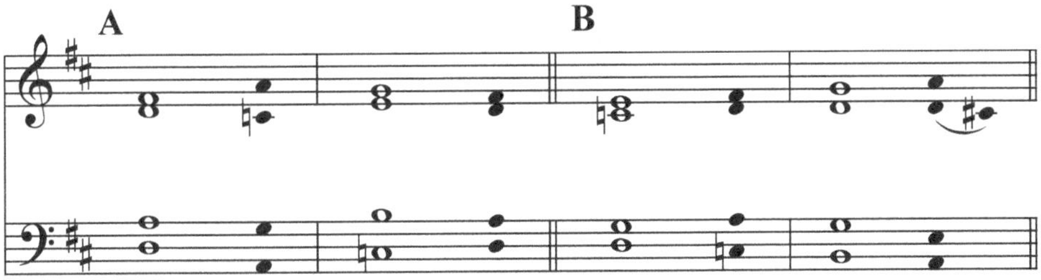

1 The LORD is my shepherd; *
I shall not be in want.
2 He makes me lie down in green pastures *
and leads me beside still waters. [ANT.]

3 He revives my soul *
and guides me along right pathways for his Name's sake.
4 Though I walk through the valley of the shadow of death,
I shall fear no evil; *
for you are with me;
your rod and your staff, they comfort me. [ANT.]

5 You spread a table before me in the presence of those
who trouble me; *
you have anointed my head with oil,
and my cup is running over.
6 Surely your goodness and mercy shall follow me all the days
of my life, *
and I will dwell in the house of the LORD for ever. [ANT.]

RCL Easter 5B **Psalm 22: 24–30**

based on "Birmingham" (H82–437)

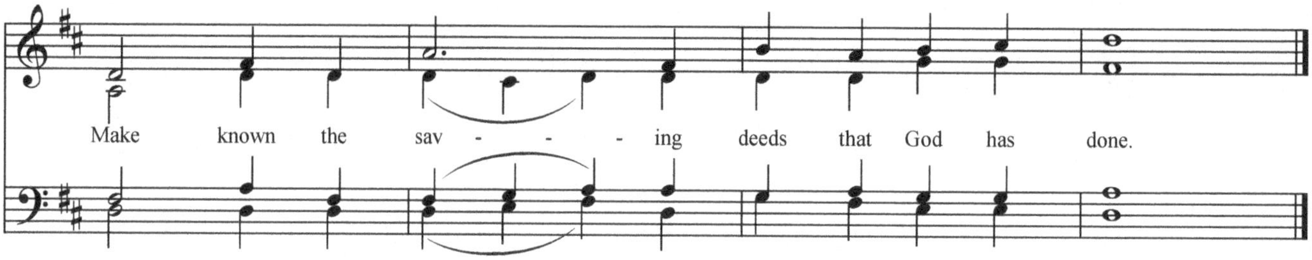

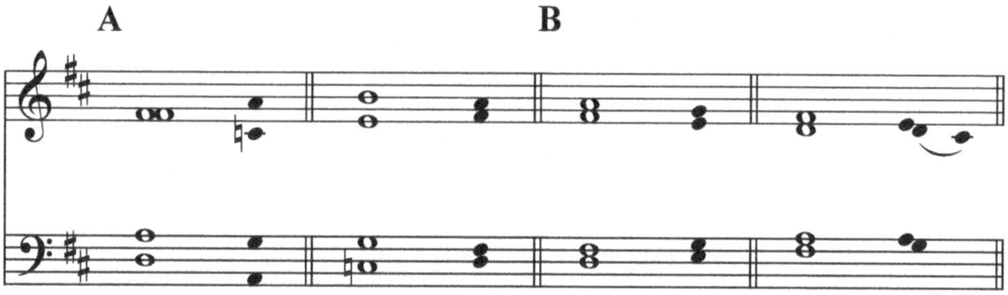

24 My praise is of him in the great assembly; *
I will perform my vows in the presence of those who worship him.
25 The poor shall eat and be satisfied,
and those who seek the LORD shall praise him: *
"May your heart live for ever!" [ANT.]

A 26 All the ends of the earth shall remember and turn to the LORD, *
and all the families of the nations shall bow before him.
A 27 For kingship belongs to the LORD; *
he rules over the nations.
B 28 To him alone all who sleep in the earth bow down in worship; *
all who go down to the dust fall before him. [ANT.]

29 My soul shall live for him;
my descendants shall serve him; *
they shall be known as the LORD's for ever.
30 They shall come and make known to a people yet unborn *
the saving deeds that he has done. [ANT.]

RCL Easter 6B Psalm 98

based on "Gelobt sei Gott" (H82–205)

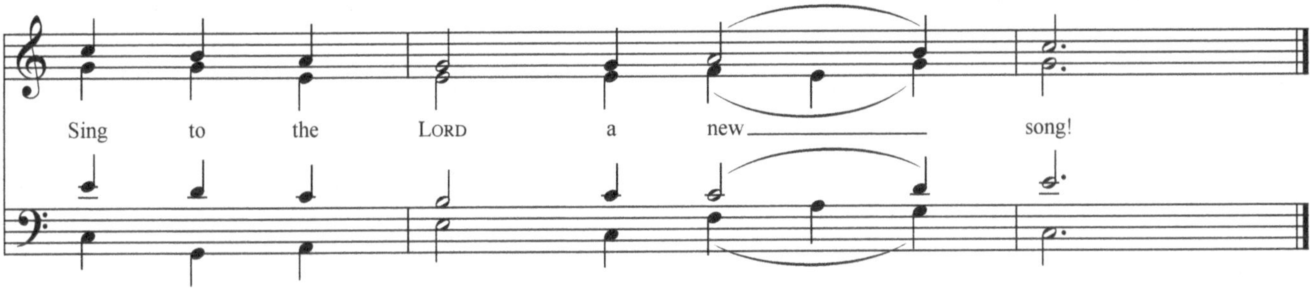

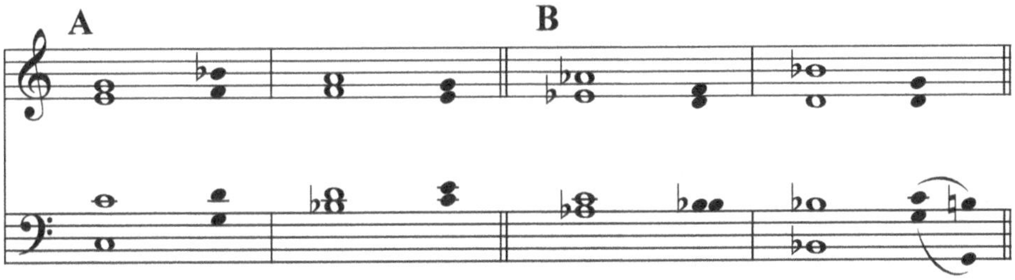

1 Sing to the LORD a new song, *
for he has done marvelous things.
2 With his right hand and his holy arm *
has he won for himself the victory. [ANT.]

3 The LORD has made known his victory; *
his righteousness has he openly shown in
the sight of the nations.
4 He remembers his mercy and faithfulness to
the house of Israel, *
and all the ends of the earth have seen the
victory of our God. [ANT.]

A 5 Shout with joy to the LORD, all you lands; *
lift up your voice, rejoice, and sing.
A 6 Sing to the LORD with the harp, *
with the harp and the voice of song.
B 7 With trumpets and the sound of the horn *
shout with joy before the King, the LORD. [ANT.]

A 8 Let the sea make a noise and all that is in it, *
the lands and those who dwell therein.
A 9 Let the rivers clap their hands, *
and let the hills ring out with joy before the LORD,
when he comes to judge the earth.
B 10 In righteousness shall he judge the world *
and the peoples with equity. [ANT.]

For

Ascension Day

see

Pages 142 – 143

RCL Easter 7B   Psalm 1

based on "Es flog ein kleins Waldvögelein" (H82–616)

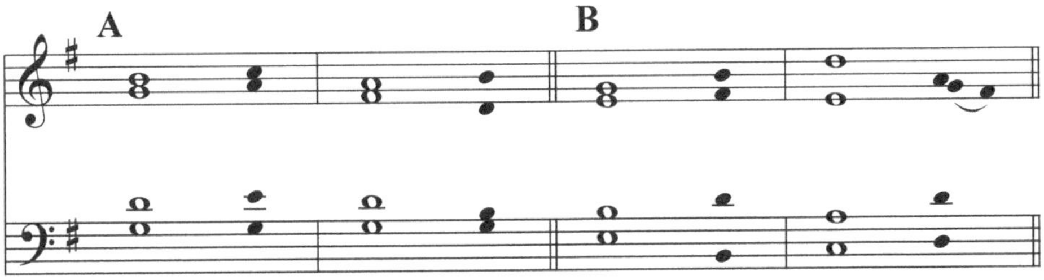

1 Happy are they who have not walked in the counsel of
the wicked, *
nor lingered in the way of sinners,
nor sat in the seats of the scornful!
2 Their delight is in the law of the LORD, *
and they meditate on his law day and night. [ANT.]

3 They are like trees planted by streams of water,
bearing fruit in due season, with leaves that do not wither; *
everything they do shall prosper.
4 It is not so with the wicked; *
they are like chaff which the wind blows away. [ANT.]

5 Therefore the wicked shall not stand upright when
judgment comes, *
nor the sinner in the council of the righteous.
6 For the LORD knows the way of the righteous, *
but the way of the wicked is doomed. [ANT.]

For
Pentecost
see
Pages 144 – 149

Year C

RCL Advent 1C **Psalm 25: 1–9**

based on "Verbum supernum prodiens" (H82–63)

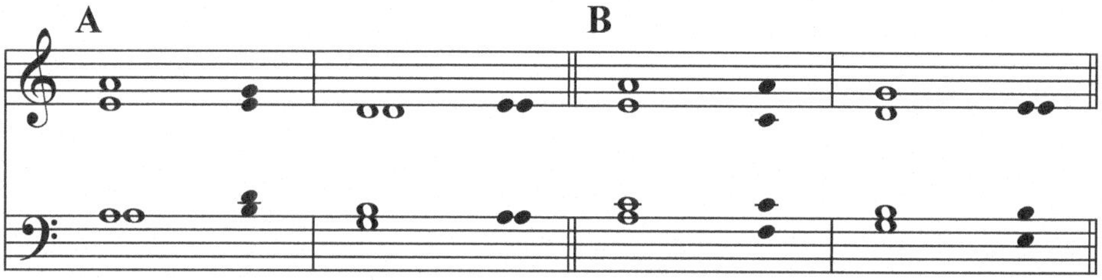

A 1 To you, O Lord, I lift up my soul;
my God, I put my trust in you; *
A let me not be humiliated,
nor let my enemies triumph over me.
B 2 Let none who look to you be put to shame; *
let the treacherous be disappointed in their schemes. [ANT.]

3 Show me your ways, O Lord, *
and teach me your paths.
4 Lead me in your truth and teach me, *
for you are the God of my salvation;
in you have I trusted all the day long. [ANT.]

5 Remember, O Lord, your compassion and love, *
for they are from everlasting.
6 Remember not the sins of my youth and my transgressions; *
remember me according to your love
and for the sake of your goodness, O Lord. [ANT.]

A 7 Gracious and upright is the Lord; *
therefore he teaches sinners in his way.
A 8 He guides the humble in doing right *
and teaches his way to the lowly.
B 9 All the paths of the Lord are love and faithfulness *
to those who keep his covenant and his testimonies. [ANT.]

RCL Advent 2C Canticle 16

based on "Bereden väg för Herran" (H82–65)

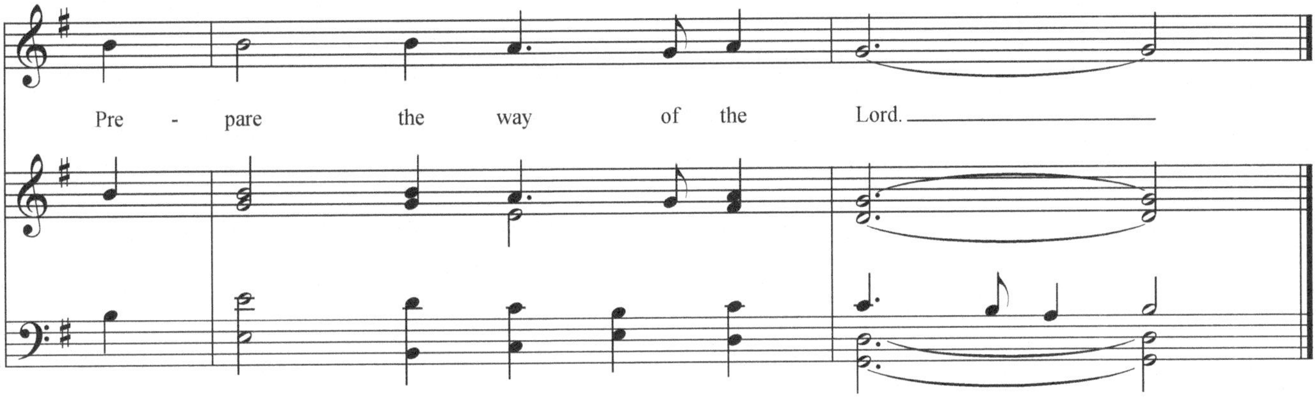

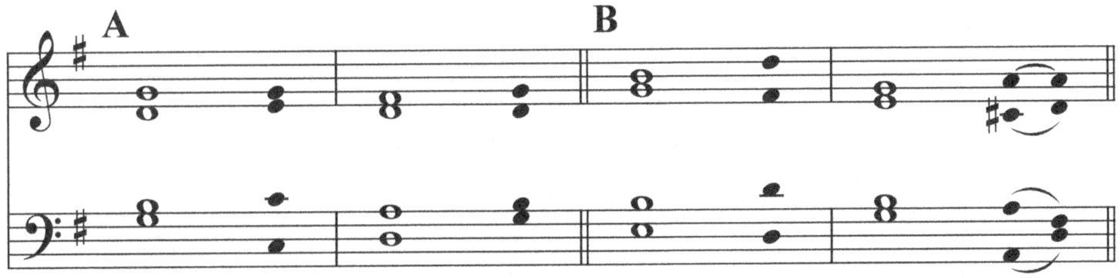

1 Blessed be the Lord, the God of Israel, *
he has come to his people and set them free.
2 He has raised up for us a mighty Savior, *
born of the house of his servant David. [ANT.]

A 3 Through his holy prophets he promised of old
that he would save us from our enemies, *
from the hands of all who hate us,
B 4 He promised to show mercy to our fathers, *
and to remember his holy covenant.
A 5 This was the oath he swore to our father Abraham, *
to set us free from the hands of our enemies,
B 6 Free to worship him without fear, *
holy and righteous in his sight
all the days of our life. [ANT.]

7 You, my child, shall be called the prophet of the Most High, *
for you will go before the Lord to prepare his way,
8 To give his people knowledge of salvation *
by the forgiveness of their sins. [ANT.]

9 In the tender compassion of our God *
the dawn from on high shall break upon us,
10 To shine on those who dwell in darkness and the shadow of death, *
and to guide our feet into the way of peace. [ANT.]

RCL Advent 3C **Canticle 9**

based on "Nun komm, der Heiden Heiland" (H82–54)

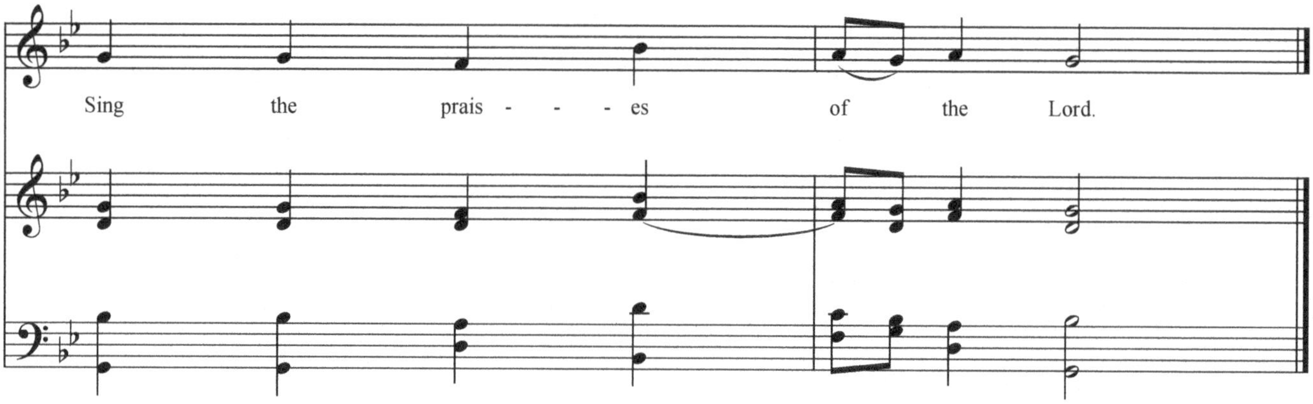

1 Surely, it is God who saves me; *
I will trust in him and not be afraid.
2 For the Lord is my stronghold and my sure defense, *
and he will be my Savior. [ANT.]

A 3 Therefore you shall draw water with rejoicing *
from the springs of salvation.
A 4 And on that day you shall say, *
Give thanks to the Lord and call upon his Name;
B 5 Make his deeds known among the peoples; *
see that they remember that his Name is exalted. [ANT.]

6 Sing the praises of the Lord, for he has done great things, *
and this is known in all the world.
7 Cry aloud, inhabitants of Zion, ring out your joy, *
for the great one in the midst of you is the Holy One of Israel. [ANT.]

RCL Advent 4C Canticle 15

based on "Birmingham" (H82–437)

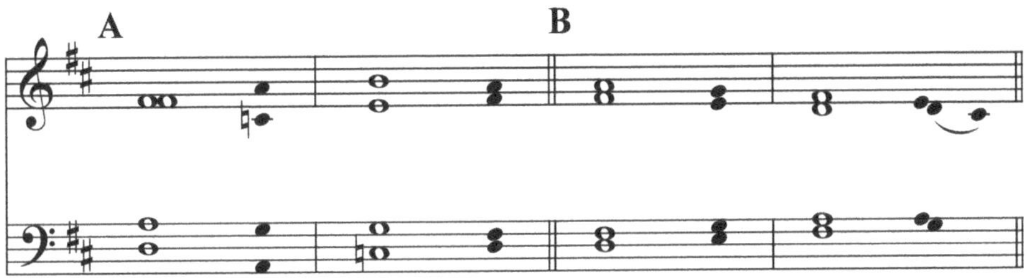

1 My soul proclaims the greatness of the Lord,
my spirit rejoices in God my Savior, *
for he has looked with favor on his lowly servant.
2 From this day all generations will call me blessed: *
the Almighty has done great things for me,
and holy is his Name. [ANT.]

3 He has mercy on those who fear him *
in every generation.
4 He has shown the strength of his arm,
he has scattered the proud in their conceit. [ANT.]

5 He has cast down the mighty from their thrones, *
and has lifted up the lowly.
6 He has filled the hungry with good things, *
and the rich he has sent away empty. [ANT.]

7 He has come to the help of his servant Israel, *
for he has remembered his promise of mercy,
8 The promise he has made to our fathers, *
to Abraham and his children for ever. [ANT.]

RCL Advent 4C **Psalm 80: 1–7**

based on "Nun komm, der Heiden Heiland" (H82–54)

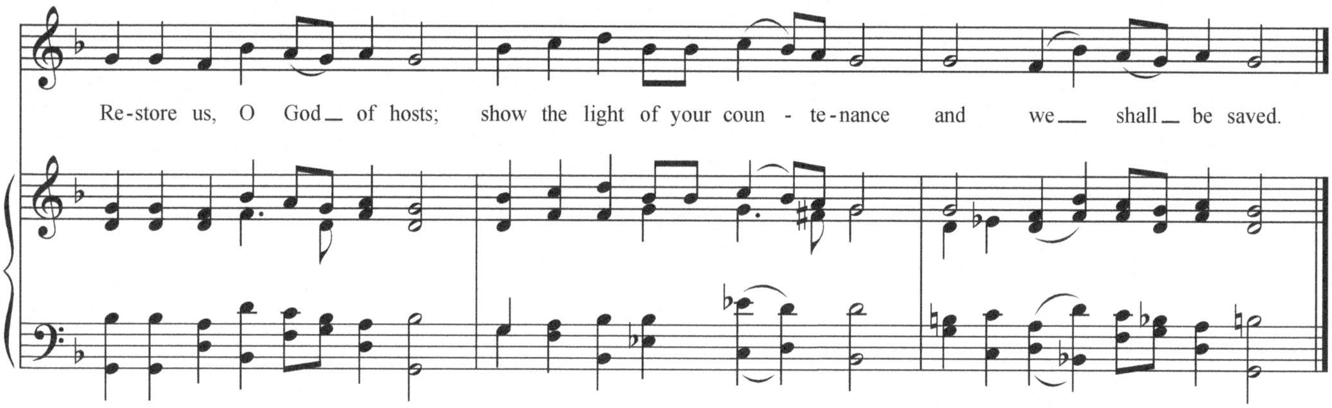

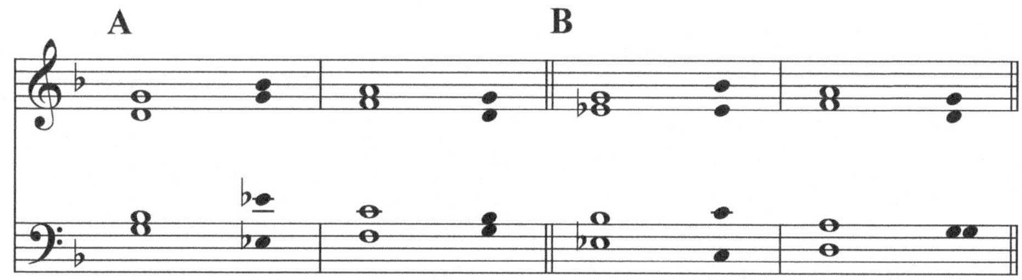

1 Hear, O Shepherd of Israel, leading Joseph like a flock; *
shine forth, you that are enthroned upon the cherubim.
2 In the presence of Ephraim, Benjamin, and Manasseh, *
stir up your strength and come to help us. [ANT.]

A 4 O Lord God of hosts, *
how long will you be angered
despite the prayers of your people?
A 5 You have fed them with the bread of tears; *
you have given them bowls of tears to drink.
B 6 You have made us the derision of our neighbors, *
and our enemies laugh us to scorn. [ANT.]

For
Christmas
through
Epiphany 1
see
Pages 98–105

RCL Epiphany 2C Psalm 36: 5–10

based on "In Babilone" (H82–437)

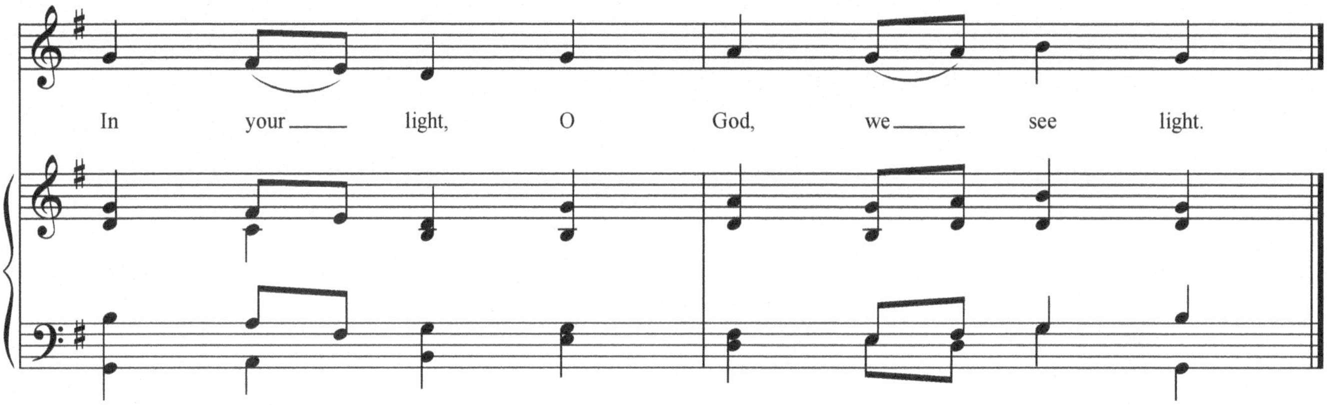

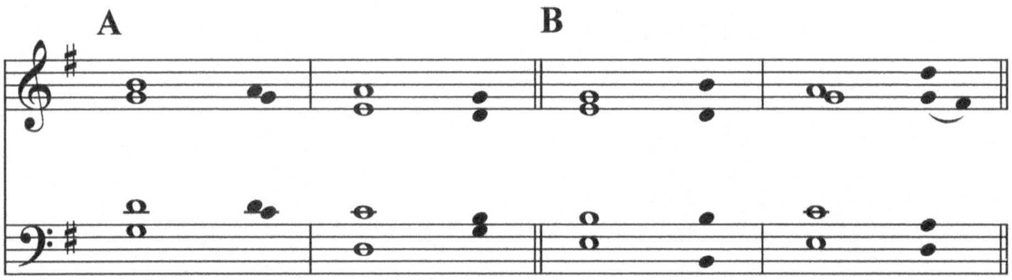

5 Your love, O LORD, reaches to the heavens, *
and your faithfulness to the clouds.
6 Your righteousness is like the strong mountains,
your justice like the great deep; *
you save both man and beast, O LORD. [ANT.]

7 How priceless is your love, O God! *
your people take refuge under the
shadow of your wings.
8 They feast upon the abundance of your house; *
you give them drink from the river of your delights. [ANT.]

9 For with you is the well of life, *
and in your light we see light.
10 Continue your loving-kindness to those who know you, *
and your favor to those who are true of heart. [ANT.]

RCL Epiphany 3C **Psalm 19**

based on "Song 1" (H82–499)

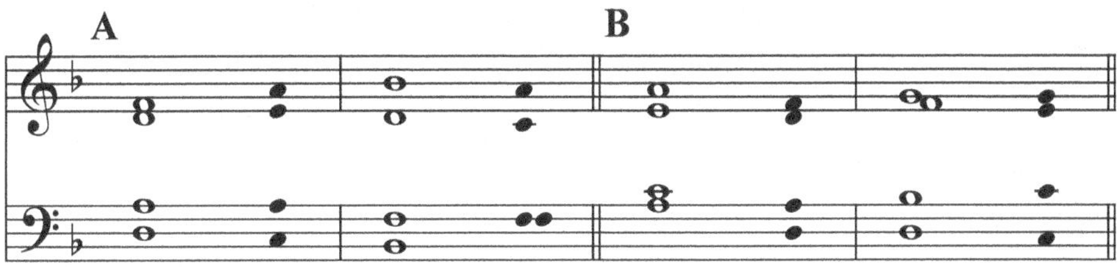

A 1 The heavens declare the glory of God, *
and the firmament shows his handiwork.
B 2 One day tells its tale to another, *
and one night imparts knowledge to another.
A 3 Although they have no words or language, *
and their voices are not heard,
B 4 Their sound has gone out into all lands, *
and their message to the ends of the world. [ANT.]

5 In the deep has he set a pavilion for the sun; *
it comes forth like a bridegroom out of his chamber;
it rejoices like a champion to run its course.
6 It goes forth from the uttermost edge of the heavens
and runs about to the end of it again; *
nothing is hidden from its burning heat. [ANT.]

7 The law of the Lord is perfect
and revives the soul; *
the testimony of the Lord is sure
and gives wisdom to the innocent.
8 The statutes of the Lord are just
and rejoice the heart; *
the commandment of the Lord is clear
and gives light to the eyes. [ANT.]

9 The fear of the Lord is clean
and endures for ever; *
the judgments of the Lord are true
and righteous altogether.
10 More to be desired are they than gold,
more than much fine gold, *
sweeter far than honey,
than honey in the comb. [ANT.]

11 By them also is your servant enlightened, *
and in keeping them there is great reward.
12 Who can tell how often he offends? *
cleanse me from my secret faults. [ANT.]

13 Above all, keep your servant from presumptuous sins;
let them not get dominion over me; *
then shall I be whole and sound,
and innocent of a great offense.
14 Let the words of my mouth and the meditation of my
heart be acceptable in your sight, *
O Lord, my strength and my redeemer. [ANT.]

RCL Epiphany 4C Psalm 71: 1–6

based on "Paderborn" (H82–535)

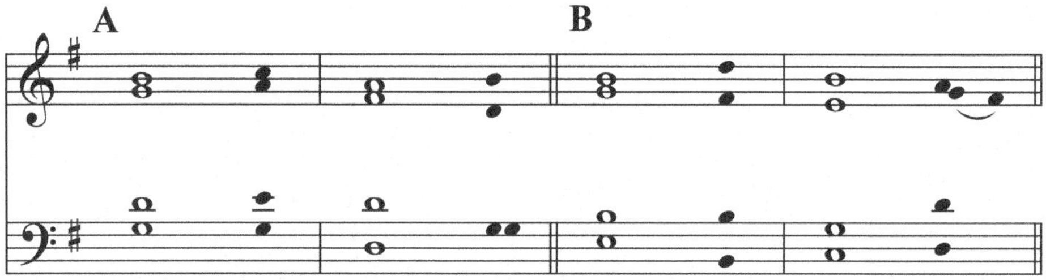

1 In you, O LORD, have I taken refuge; *
let me never be ashamed.
2 In your righteousness, deliver me and set me free; *
incline your ear to me and save me. [ANT.]

3 Be my strong rock, a castle to keep me safe; *
you are my crag and my stronghold.
4 Deliver me, my God, from the hand of the wicked, *
from the clutches of the evildoer and the oppressor. [ANT.]

5 For you are my hope, O Lord GOD, *
my confidence since I was young.
6 I have been sustained by you ever since I was born;
from my mother's womb you have been my strength; *
my praise shall be always of you. [ANT.]

For
The Presentation, February 2
see
Page 106 – 107

RCL Epiphany 5C Psalm 138

based on "Ton-y-Botel" (H82–381)

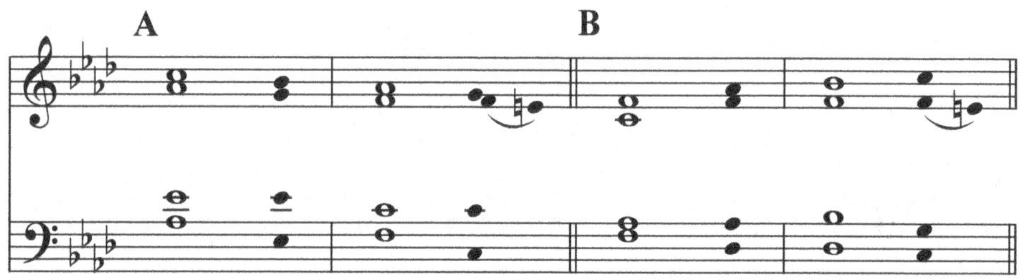

A 1 I will give thanks to you, O LORD, with my whole heart; *
before the gods I will sing your praise.
A 2 I will bow down toward your holy temple
and praise your Name, *
because of your love and faithfulness;
B 3 For you have glorified your Name *
and your word above all things. [ANT.]

A 4 When I called, you answered me; *
you increased my strength within me.
A 5 All the kings of the earth will praise you, O LORD, *
when they have heard the words of your mouth.
B 6 They will sing of the ways of the LORD, *
that great is the glory of the LORD. [ANT.]

A 7 Though the LORD be high, he cares for the lowly; *
he perceives the haughty from afar.
A 8 Though I walk in the midst of trouble, you keep me safe; *
you stretch forth your hand against the fury of my enemies;
your right hand shall save me.
B 9 The LORD will make good his purpose for me; *
O LORD, your love endures for ever;
do not abandon the works of your hands. [ANT.]

RCL Epiphany 6C **Psalm 1**

based on "Old 100th" (H82–377)

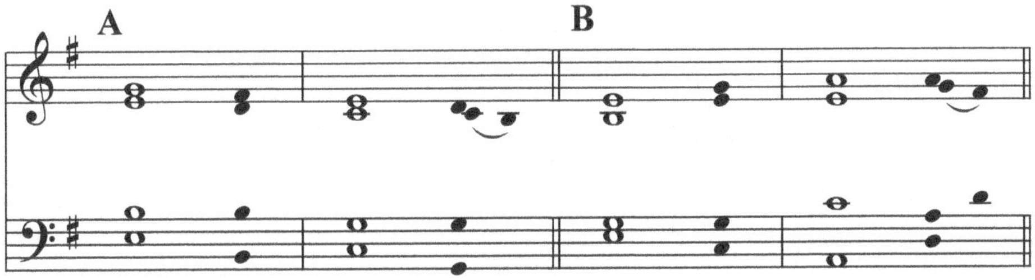

1 Happy are they who have not walked in the counsel of
the wicked, *
nor lingered in the way of sinners,
nor sat in the seats of the scornful!
2 Their delight is in the law of the LORD, *
and they meditate on his law day and night. [ANT.]

3 They are like trees planted by streams of water,
bearing fruit in due season, with leaves that do not wither; *
everything they do shall prosper.
4 It is not so with the wicked; *
they are like chaff which the wind blows away. [ANT.]

5 Therefore the wicked shall not stand upright when
judgment comes, *
nor the sinner in the council of the righteous.
6 For the LORD knows the way of the righteous, *
but the way of the wicked is doomed. [ANT.]

RCL Epiphany 7C Psalm 37: 1–12, 41–42

based on "O quanta qualia" (H82–348)

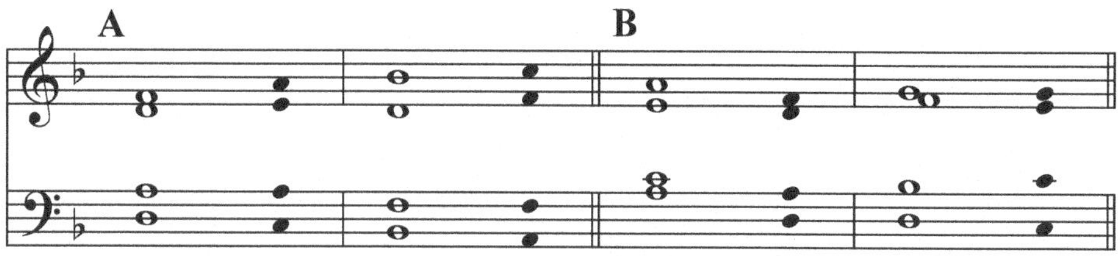

1 Do not fret yourself because of evildoers; *
do not be jealous of those who do wrong.
2 For they shall soon wither like the grass, *
and like the green grass fade away. [ANT.]

A 3 Put your trust in the LORD and do good; *
dwell in the land and feed on its riches.
B 4 Take delight in the LORD, *
and he shall give you your heart's desire.
A 5 Commit your way to the LORD and put your trust in him, *
and he will bring it to pass.
B 6 He will make your righteousness as clear as the light *
and your just dealing as the noonday. [ANT.]

A 7 Be still before the LORD *
and wait patiently for him.
B 8 Do not fret yourself over the one who prospers, *
the one who succeeds in evil schemes.
A 9 Refrain from anger, leave rage alone; *
do not fret yourself; it leads only to evil.
B 10 For evildoers shall be cut off, *
but those who wait upon the LORD shall possess the land. [ANT.]

11 In a little while the wicked shall be no more; *
you shall search out their place, but they will not be there.
12 But the lowly shall possess the land; *
they will delight in abundance of peace. [ANT.]

41 But the deliverance of the righteous comes from the LORD; *
he is their stronghold in time of trouble.
42 The LORD will help them and rescue them; *
he will rescue them from the wicked and deliver them,
because they seek refuge in him. [ANT.]

RCL Epiphany 8C **Psalm 92: 1–4, 11–14**

based on "Rouen" (H82–360)

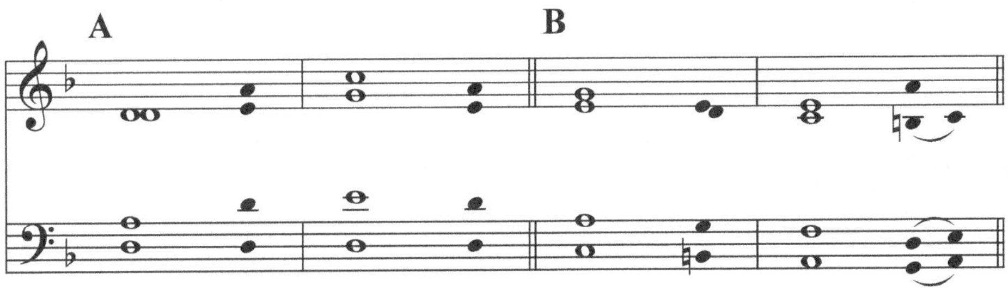

A 1 It is a good thing to give thanks to the LORD, *
and to sing praises to your Name, O Most High;
B 2 To tell of your loving-kindness early in the morning *
and of your faithfulness in the night season;
A 3 On the psaltery, and on the lyre, *
and to the melody of the harp.
B 4 For you have made me glad by your acts, O LORD; *
and I shout for joy because of the works of your hands. [ANT.]

11 The righteous shall flourish like a palm tree, *
and shall spread abroad like a cedar of Lebanon.
12 Those who are planted in the house of the LORD *
shall flourish in the courts of our God; [ANT.]

13 They shall still bear fruit in old age; *
they shall be green and succulent;
14 That they may show how upright the LORD is, *
my Rock, in whom there is no fault. [ANT.]

RCL Epiphany Last C Psalm 99

based on "Old 124th" (H82–149)

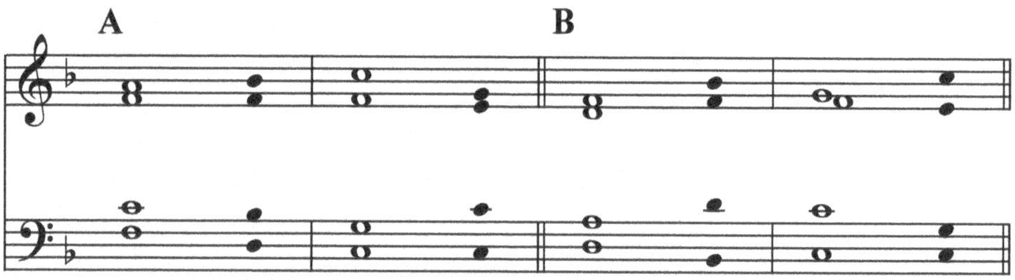

A 1 The LORD is King;
let the people tremble; *
he is enthroned upon the cherubim;
let the earth shake.
A 2 The LORD is great in Zion; *
he is high above all peoples.
B 3 Let them confess his Name, which is great and awesome; *
he is the Holy One. [ANT.]

4 "O mighty King, lover of justice,
you have established equity; *
you have executed justice and righteousness in Jacob."
5 Proclaim the greatness of the LORD our God
and fall down before his footstool; *
he is the Holy One. [ANT.]

6 Moses and Aaron among his priests,
and Samuel among those who call upon his Name, *
they called upon the LORD, and he answered them.
7 He spoke to them out of the pillar of cloud; *
they kept his testimonies and the decree that he gave them. [ANT.]

8 "O LORD our God, you answered them indeed; *
you were a God who forgave them,
yet punished them for their evil deeds."
9 Proclaim the greatness of the LORD our God
and worship him upon his holy hill; *
for the LORD our God is the Holy One. [ANT.]

For
Ash Wednesday
see
Page 108

RCL Lent 1C Psalm 91: 1–2, 9–16

based on "A la venue de Noël" (H82–152)

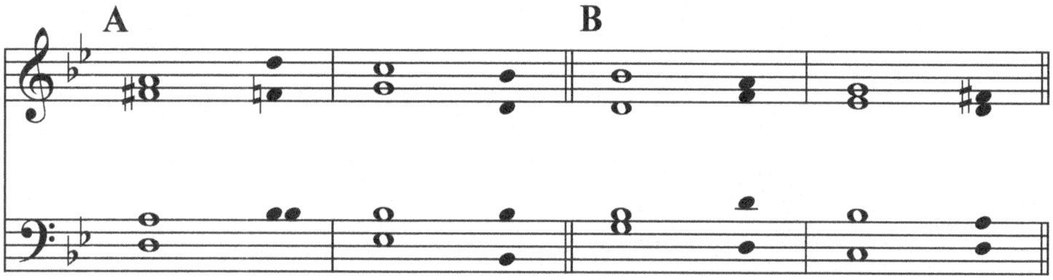

1 He who dwells in the shelter of the Most High, *
abides under the shadow of the Almighty.
2 He shall say to the LORD,
"You are my refuge and my stronghold, *
my God in whom I put my trust." [ANT.]

9 Because you have made the LORD your refuge, *
and the Most High your habitation,
10 There shall no evil happen to you, *
neither shall any plague come near your dwelling. [ANT.]

A 11 For he shall give his angels charge over you, *
to keep you in all your ways.
A 12 They shall bear you in their hands, *
lest you dash your foot against a stone.
B 13 You shall tread upon the lion and adder; *
you shall trample the young lion and the serpent
under your feet. [ANT.]

A 14 Because he is bound to me in love,
therefore will I deliver him; *
I will protect him, because he knows my Name.
A 15 He shall call upon me, and I will answer him; *
I am with him in trouble;
I will rescue him and bring him to honor.
B 16 With long life will I satisfy him, *
and show him my salvation. [ANT.]

RCL Lent 2C **Psalm 27**

based on "Es flog ein kleins Waldvögelein" (H82–48)

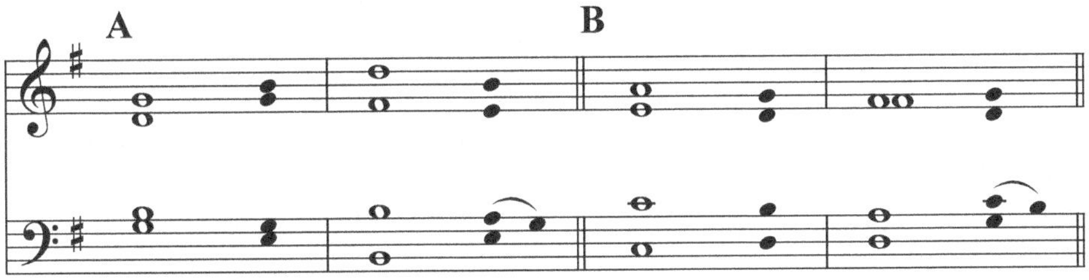

1 The Lord is my light and my salvation;
whom then shall I fear? *
the Lord is the strength of my life;
of whom then shall I be afraid? [ANT.]

A 2 When evildoers came upon me to eat up my flesh, *
it was they, my foes and my adversaries, who stumbled and fell.
A 3 Though an army should encamp against me, *
yet my heart shall not be afraid;
B 4 And though war should rise up against me, *
yet will I put my trust in him. [ANT.]

5 One thing have I asked of the Lord;
one thing I seek; *
that I may dwell in the house of the Lord all the days of my life;
6 To behold the fair beauty of the Lord *
and to seek him in his temple. [ANT.]

A 7 For in the day of trouble he shall keep me safe in his shelter; *
he shall hide me in the secrecy of his dwelling
and set me high upon a rock.
A 8 Even now he lifts up my head *
above my enemies round about me.
B 9 Therefore I will offer in his dwelling an oblation
with sounds of great gladness; *
I will sing and make music to the Lord. [ANT.]

10 Hearken to my voice, O Lord, when I call; *
have mercy on me and answer me.
11 You speak in my heart and say, "Seek my face." *
Your face, Lord, will I seek. [ANT.]

A 12 Hide not your face from me, *
nor turn away your servant in displeasure.
A 13 You have been my helper;
cast me not away; *
do not forsake me, O God of my salvation.
B 14 Though my father and my mother forsake me, *
the Lord will sustain me. [ANT.]

15 Show me your way, O Lord; *
lead me on a level path, because of my enemies.
16 Deliver me not into the hand of my adversaries, *
for false witnesses have risen up against me,
and also those who speak malice. [ANT.]

17 What if I had not believed
that I should see the goodness of the Lord *
in the land of the living!
18 O tarry and await the Lord's pleasure;
be strong, and he shall comfort your heart; *
wait patiently for the Lord. [ANT.]

RCL Lent 3C Psalm 63: 1–8

based on "Wondrous Love" (H82–439)

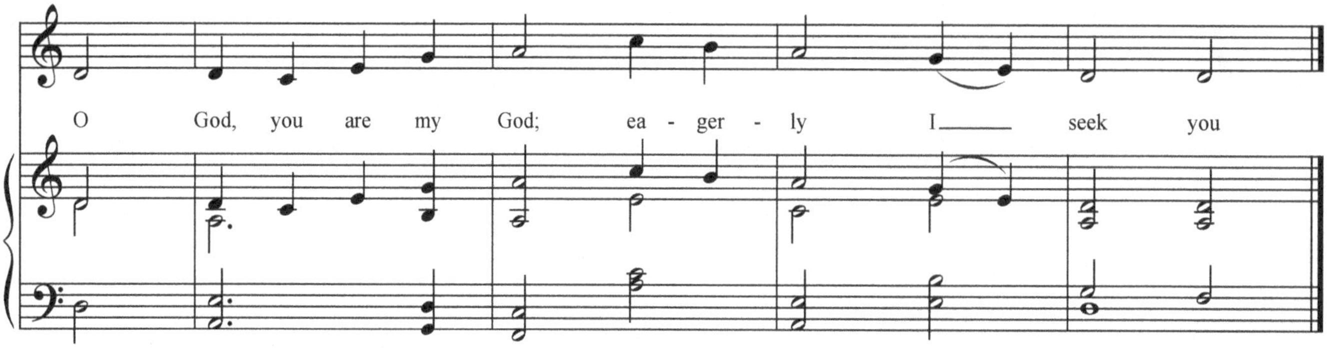

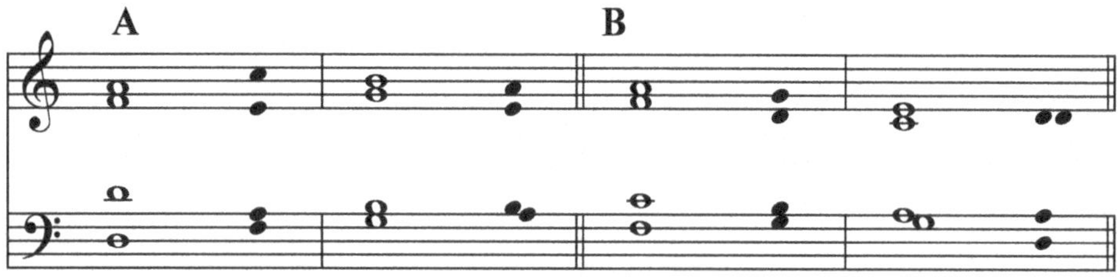

1 O God, you are my God; eagerly I seek you; *
my soul thirsts for you, my flesh faints for you,
as in a barren and dry land where there is no water.
2 Therefore I have gazed upon you in your holy place, *
that I might behold your power and your glory. [ANT.]

3 For your loving-kindness is better than life itself; *
my lips shall give you praise.
4 So will I bless you as long as I live *
and lift up my hands in your Name. [ANT.]

5 My soul is content, as with marrow and fatness, *
and my mouth praises you with joyful lips,
6 When I remember you upon my bed, *
and meditate on you in the night watches. [ANT.]

7 For you have been my helper, *
and under the shadow of your wings I will rejoice.
8 My soul clings to you; *
your right hand holds me fast. [ANT.]

RCL Lent 4C Psalm 32

based on "Tender Thought" (H82–702)

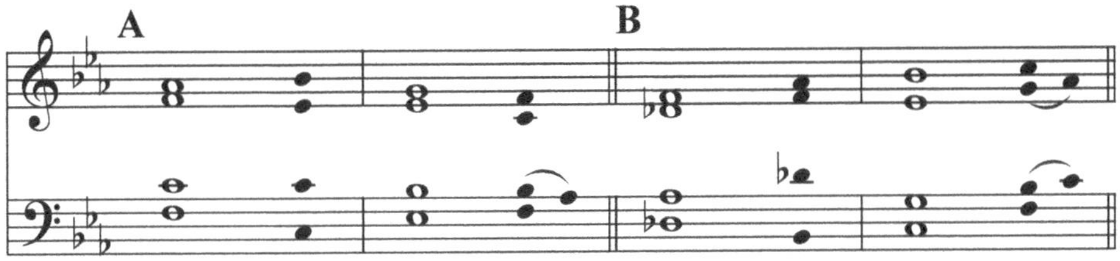

1 Happy are they whose transgressions are forgiven, *
and whose sin is put away!
2 Happy are they to whom the LORD imputes no guilt, *
and in whose spirit there is no guile! [ANT.]

3 While I held my tongue, my bones withered away, *
because of my groaning all day long.
4 For your hand was heavy upon me day and night; *
my moisture was dried up as in the heat of summer. [ANT.]

5 Then I acknowledged my sin to you, *
and did not conceal my guilt.
6 I said, "I will confess my transgressions to the LORD." *
Then you forgave me the guilt of my sin. [ANT.]

7 Therefore all the faithful will make their prayers to you in time of trouble; *
when the great waters overflow, they shall not reach them.
8 You are my hiding-place;
you preserve me from trouble; *
you surround me with shouts of deliverance. [ANT.]

9 "I will instruct you and teach you in the way that you should go; *
I will guide you with my eye.
10 Do not be like horse or mule, which have no understanding; *
who must be fitted with bit and bridle,
or else they will not stay near you." [ANT.]

11 Great are the tribulations of the wicked; *
but mercy embraces those who trust in the LORD.
12 Be glad, you righteous, and rejoice in the LORD; *
shout for joy, all who are true of heart. [ANT.]

RCL Lent 5C Psalm 126

based on "New Britain" (H82–671)

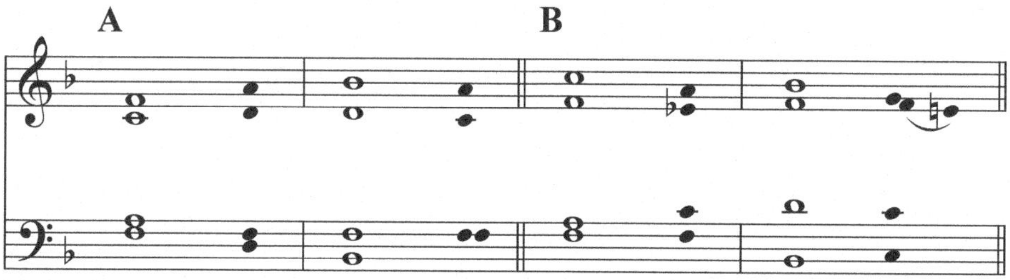

1 When the LORD restored the fortunes of Zion, *
then were we like those who dream.
2 Then was our mouth filled with laughter, *
and our tongue with shouts of joy. [ANT.]

3 Then they said among the nations, *
"The LORD has done great things for them."
5 Restore our fortunes, O LORD, *
like the watercourses of the Negev. [ANT.]

6 Those who sowed with tears *
will reap with songs of joy.
7 Those who go out weeping, carrying the seed, *
will come again with joy, shouldering their sheaves. [ANT.]

For
Palm Sunday
through
Easter Week
see
Pages 110 – 141

RCL Easter 2C Psalm 118: 14–29

based on "Vruechten" (H82–192)

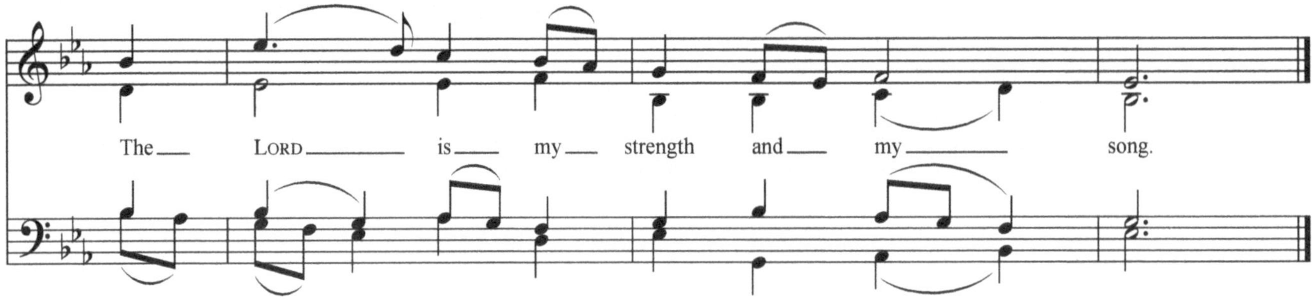

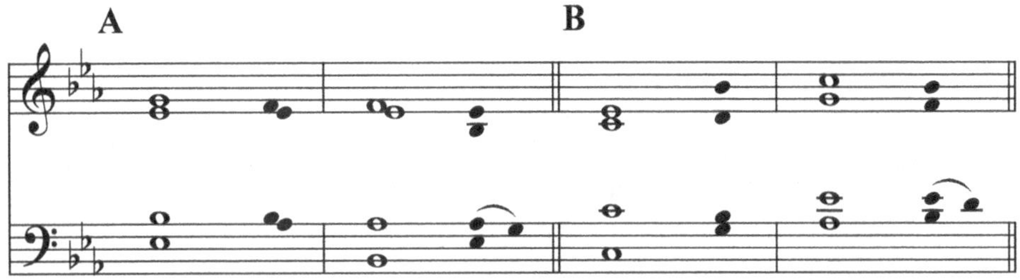

A 14 The LORD is my strength and my song, *
and he has become my salvation.
A 15 There is a sound of exultation and victory *
in the tents of the righteous:
B 16 "The right hand of the LORD has triumphed! *
the right hand of the LORD is exalted!
the right hand of the LORD has triumphed!" [ANT.]

17 I shall not die, but live, *
and declare the works of the LORD.
18 The Lord has punished me sorely, *
but he did not hand me over to death. [ANT.]

A 19 Open for me the gates of righteousness; *
I will enter them;
I will offer thanks to the LORD.
A 20 "This is the gate of the LORD; *
he who is righteous may enter."
B 21 I will give thanks to you, for you answered me *
and have become my salvation. [ANT.]

A 22 The same stone which the builders rejected *
has become the chief cornerstone.
A 23 This is the LORD's doing, *
and it is marvelous in our eyes.
B 24 On this day the LORD has acted; *
we will rejoice and be glad in it. [ANT.]

25 Hosannah, LORD, hosannah! *
LORD, send us now success.
26 Blessed is he who comes in the name of the LORD; *
we bless you from the house of the LORD. [ANT.]

A 27 God is the LORD; he has shined upon us; *
form a procession with branches up to
the horns of the altar.
A 28 "You are my God, and I will thank you; *
you are my God, and I will exalt you."
B 29 Give thanks to the LORD, for he is good; *
his mercy endures for ever. [ANT.]

RCL Easter 2C Psalm 150

based on "Salvation" (H82–243)

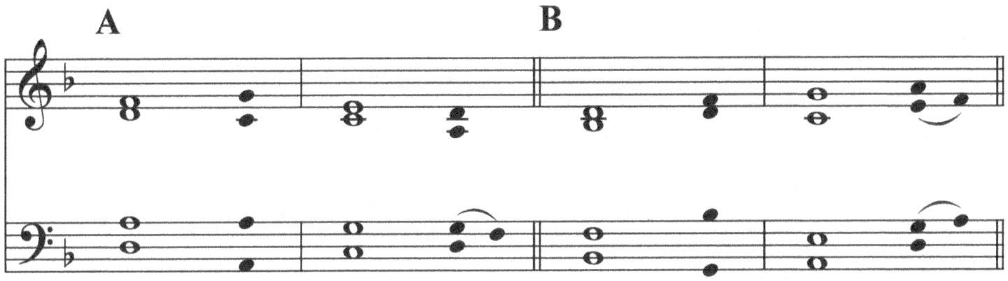

1 Hallelujah!
Praise God in his holy temple; *
praise him in the firmament of his power.
2 Praise him for his mighty acts; *
praise him for his excellent greatness. [ANT.]

3 Praise him with the blast of the ram's-horn; *
praise him with lyre and harp.
4 Praise him with timbrel and dance; *
praise him with strings and pipe. [ANT.]

5 Praise him with resounding cymbals; *
praise him with loud-clanging cymbals.
6 Let everything that has breath *
praise the LORD.
Hallelujah! [ANT.]

RCL Easter 3C Psalm 30

based on "Truro" (H82–182)

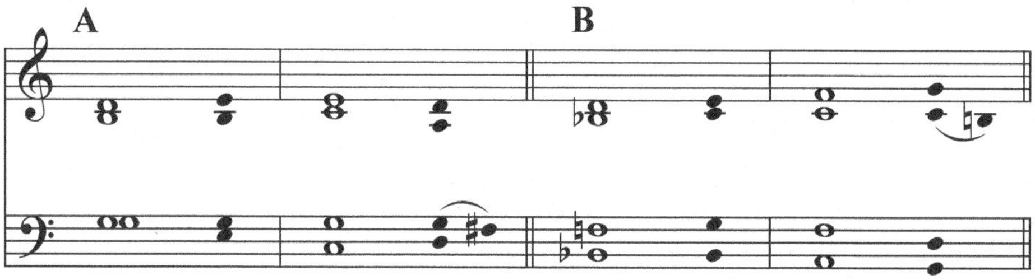

A 1 I will exalt you, O LORD,
because you have lifted me up *
and have not let my enemies triumph over me.
A 2 O LORD my God, I cried out to you, *
and you restored me to health.
B 3 You brought me up, O LORD, from the dead; *
you restored my life as I was going down to the grave. [ANT.]

A 4 Sing to the LORD, you servants of his; *
give thanks for the remembrance of his holiness.
A 5 For his wrath endures but the twinkling of an eye, *
his favor for a lifetime.
B 6 Weeping may spend the night, *
but joy comes in the morning. [ANT.]

7 While I felt secure, I said,
"I shall never be disturbed. *
You, LORD, with your favor, made me as strong as
the mountains."
8 Then you hid your face, *
and I was filled with fear. [ANT.]

A 9 I cried to you, O LORD; *
I pleaded with the LORD, saying,
A 10 "What profit is there in my blood, if I go down to the Pit? *
will the dust praise you or declare your faithfulness?
B 11 Hear, O LORD, and have mercy upon me; *
O LORD, be my helper." [ANT.]

12 You have turned my wailing into dancing; *
you have put off my sack-cloth and clothed me with joy.
13 Therefore my heart sings to you without ceasing; *
O LORD my God, I will give you thanks for ever. [ANT.]

RCL Easter 4C Psalm 23

based on "St. Columba" (H82–645)

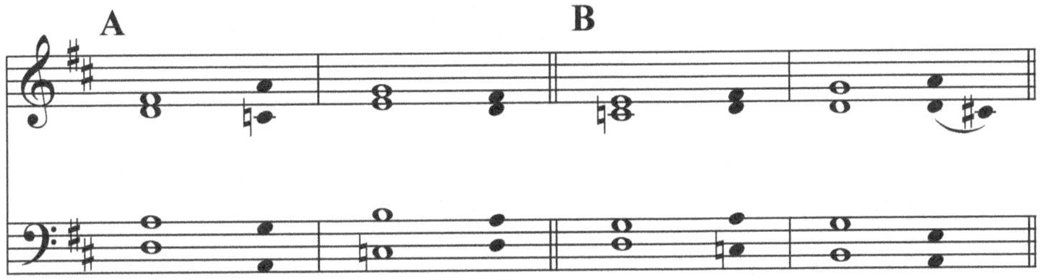

1 The LORD is my shepherd; *
I shall not be in want.
2 He makes me lie down in green pastures *
and leads me beside still waters. [ANT.]

3 He revives my soul *
and guides me along right pathways for his Name's sake.
4 Though I walk through the valley of the shadow of death,
I shall fear no evil; *
for you are with me;
your rod and your staff, they comfort me. [ANT.]

5 You spread a table before me in the presence of those
who trouble me; *
you have anointed my head with oil,
and my cup is running over.
6 Surely your goodness and mercy shall follow me all the days
of my life, *
and I will dwell in the house of the LORD for ever. [ANT.]

RCL Easter 5C   Psalm 148

based on "Gelobt sei Gott" (H82–205)

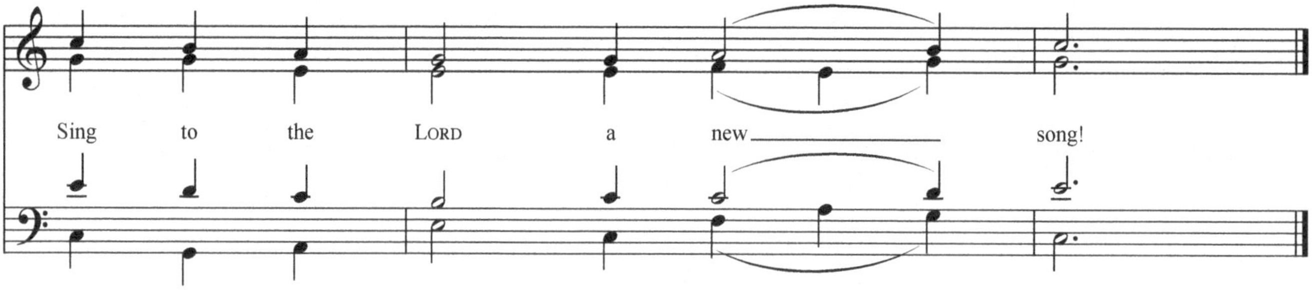

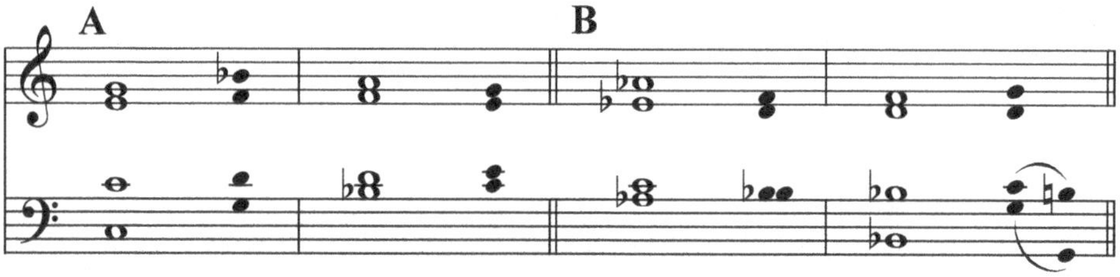

A 1 Hallelujah!
Praise the LORD from the heavens; *
praise him in the heights.
A 2 Praise him, all you angels of his; *
praise him, all his host.
B 3 Praise him, sun and moon; *
praise him, all you shining stars. [ANT.]

A 4 Praise him, heaven of heavens, *
and you waters above the heavens.
A 5 Let them praise the Name of the LORD; *
for he commanded, and they were created.
B 6 He made them stand fast for ever and ever; *
he gave them a law which shall not pass away. [ANT.]

A 7 Praise the LORD from the earth, *
you sea-monsters and all deeps;
B 8 Fire and hail, snow and fog, *
tempestuous wind, doing his will;
A 9 Mountains and all hills, *
fruit trees and all cedars;
B 10 Wild beasts and all cattle, *
creeping things and wingèd birds; [ANT.]

11 Kings of the earth and all peoples, *
princes and all rulers of the world;
12 Young men and maidens, *
old and young together. [ANT.]

13 Let them praise the Name of the LORD, *
for his Name only is exalted,
his splendor is over earth and heaven.
14 He has raised up strength for his people
and praise for all his loyal servants, *
the children of Israel, a people who are near him.
Hallelujah! [ANT.]

RCL Easter 6C Psalm 67

based on "In Babilone" (H82–215)

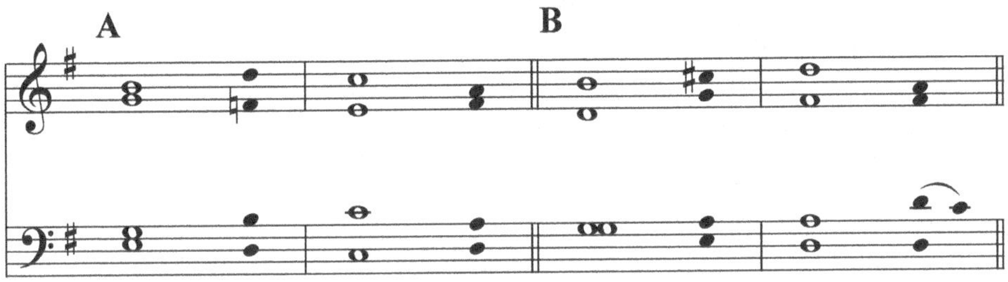

1 May God be merciful to us and bless us, *
show us the light of his countenance and come to us.
2 Let your ways be known upon earth, *
your saving health among all nations. [ANT.]

4 Let the nations be glad and sing for joy, *
for you judge the peoples with equity
and guide all the nations upon earth.
5 Let the peoples praise you, O God; *
let all the peoples praise you. [ANT.]

6 The earth has brought forth her increase; *
may God, our own God, give us his blessing.
7 May God give us his blessing, *
and may all the ends of the earth stand in awe of him. [ANT.]

For
Ascension Day
see
Pages 142 – 143

RCL Easter 7C Psalm 97

based on "Hanover" (H82–388)

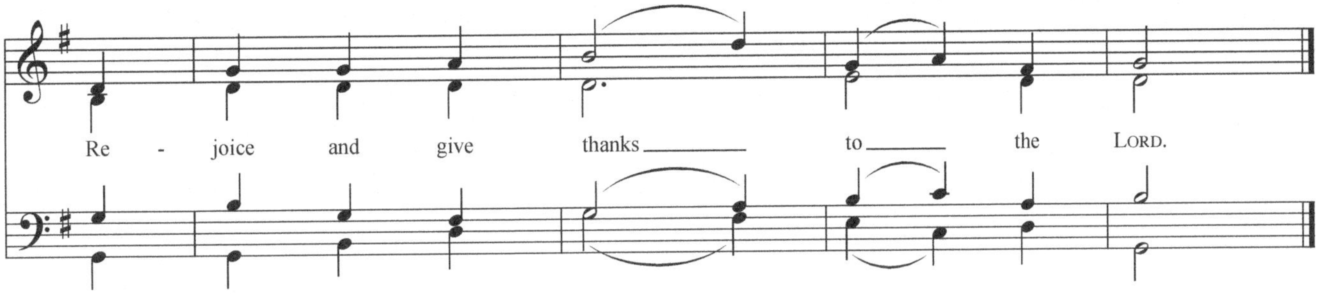

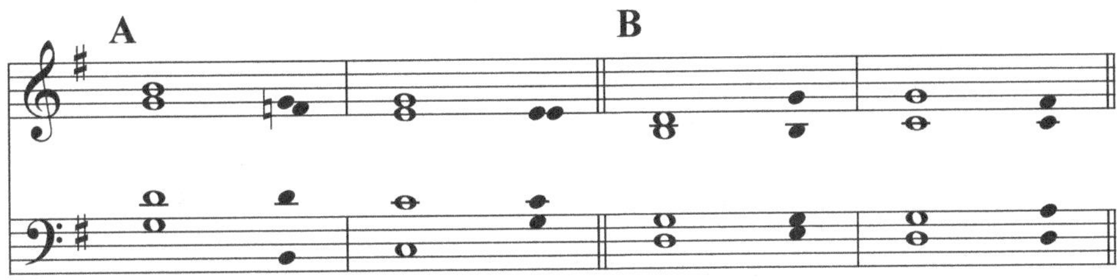

1 The LORD is King;
let the earth rejoice; *
let the multitude of the isles be glad.
2 Clouds and darkness are round about him, *
righteousness and justice are the foundations of his throne. [ANT.]

3 A fire goes before him *
and burns up his enemies on every side.
4 His lightnings light up the world; *
the earth sees it and is afraid.
5 The mountains melt like wax at the presence of the LORD, *
at the presence of the LORD of the whole earth.
6 The heavens declare his righteousness, *
and all the peoples see his glory. [ANT.]

7 Confounded be all who worship carved images
and delight in false gods! *
Bow down before him, all you gods.
8 Zion hears and is glad, and the cities of Judah rejoice, *
because of your judgments, O LORD. [ANT.]

9 For you are the LORD,
most high over all the earth; *
you are exalted far above all gods.
10 The LORD loves those who hate evil; *
he preserves the lives of his saints
and delivers them from the hand of the wicked. [ANT.]

11 Light has sprung up for the righteous, *
and joyful gladness for those who are truehearted.
12 Rejoice in the LORD, you righteous, *
and give thanks to his holy Name. [ANT.]

For
Pentecost
see
Pages 144 – 149

ABC Material

RCL Christmas Day I ABC Psalm 96

based on "Von Himmel hoch" (H82–80)

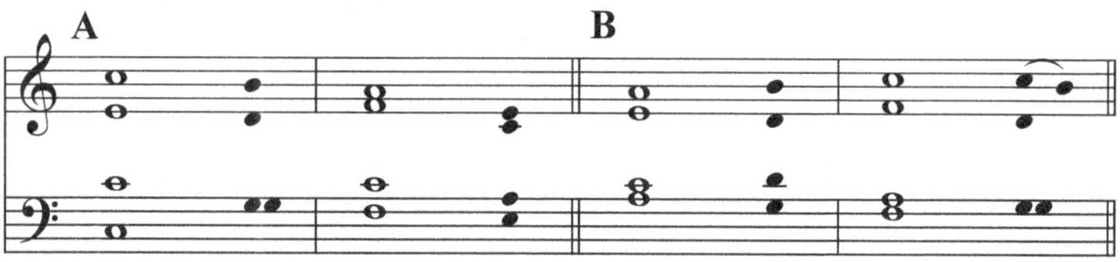

A 1 Sing to the LORD a new song; *
   sing to the LORD, all the whole earth.
B 2 Sing to the LORD and bless his Name; *
   proclaim the good news of his salvation from day to day.
A 3 Declare his glory among the nations *
   and his wonders among all peoples.
B 4 For great is the LORD and greatly to be praised; *
   he is more to be feared than all gods. [ANT.]

A 5 As for all the gods of the nations, they are but idols; *
   but it is the LORD who made the heavens.
B 6 Oh, the majesty and magnificence of his presence! *
   Oh, the power and the splendor of his sanctuary!
A 7 Ascribe to the LORD, you families of the peoples; *
   ascribe to the LORD honor and power.
B 8 Ascribe to the LORD the honor due his Name; *
   bring offerings and come into his courts. [ANT.]

9 Worship the LORD in the beauty of holiness; *
   let the whole earth tremble before him.
10 Tell it out among the nations: "The LORD is King! *
   he has made the world so firm that it cannot be moved;
   he will judge the peoples with equity." [ANT.]

A 11 Let the heavens rejoice, and let the earth be glad;
let the sea thunder and all that is in it; *
   let the field be joyful and all that is therein.
A 12 Then shall all the trees of the wood shout for joy
before the LORD when he comes, *
   when he comes to judge the earth.
B 13 He will judge the world with righteousness *
   and the peoples with his truth. [ANT.]

RCL Christmas Day II ABC Psalm 97

based on "Puer nobis nascitur" (H82–98)

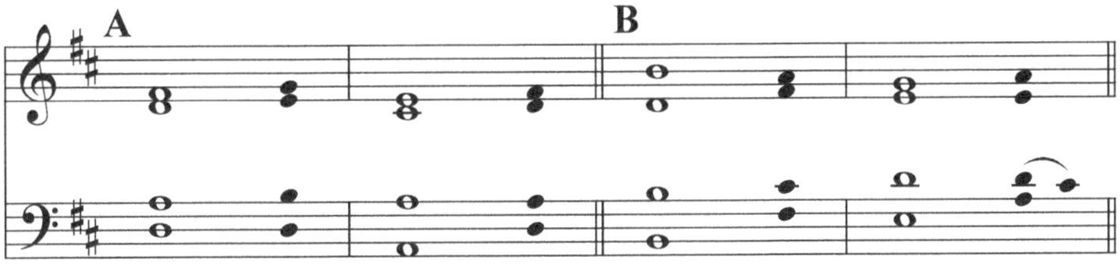

1 The LORD is King;
let the earth rejoice; *
  let the multitude of the isles be glad.
2 Clouds and darkness are round about him, *
  righteousness and justice are the foundations of his throne. [ANT.]

A 3 A fire goes before him *
  and burns up his enemies on every side.
B 4 His lightnings light up the world; *
  the earth sees it and is afraid.
A 5 The mountains melt like wax at the presence of the LORD, *
  at the presence of the LORD of the whole earth.
B 6 The heavens declare his righteousness, *
  and all the peoples see his glory. [ANT.]

A 7 Confounded be all who worship carved images
and delight in false gods! *
  Bow down before him, all you gods.
A 8 Zion hears and is glad, and the cities of Judah rejoice, *
  because of your judgments, O LORD.
B 9 For you are the LORD,
most high over all the earth; *
  you are exalted far above all gods. [ANT.]
A 10
The LORD loves those who hate evil; *
  he preserves the lives of his saints
A 11 and delivers them from the hand of the wicked.
Light has sprung up for the righteous, *
B 12 and joyful gladness for those who are truehearted.
Rejoice in the LORD, you righteous, *
  and give thanks to his holy Name. [ANT.]

RCL Christmas Day III ABC **Psalm 98**

based on "Antioch" (H82–100)

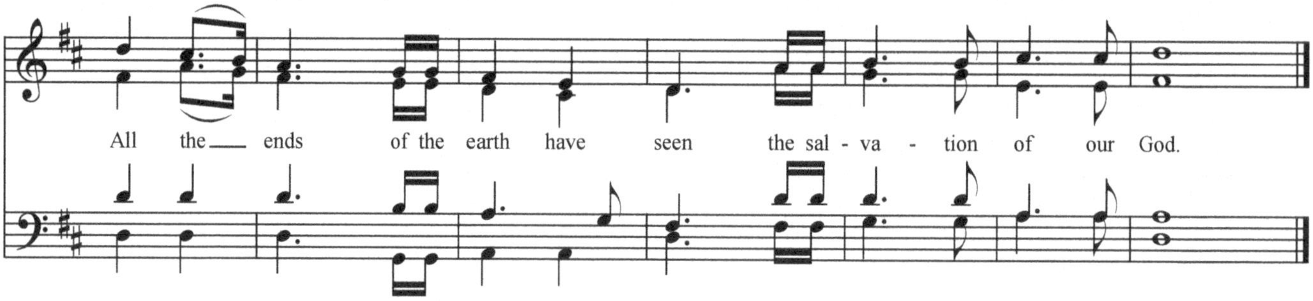

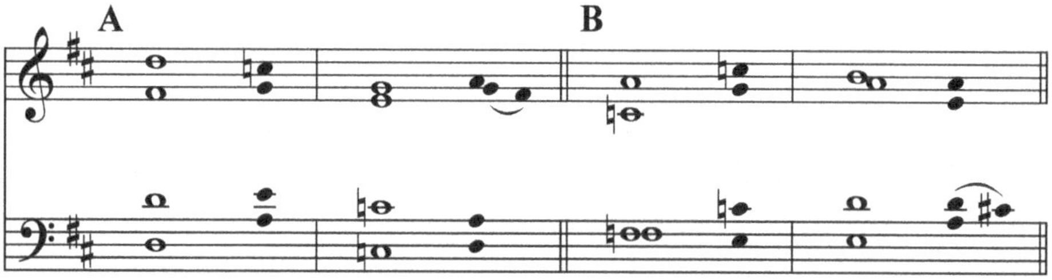

A 1 Sing to the LORD a new song, * for he has done marvelous things.

B 2 With his right hand and his holy arm * has he won for himself the victory.

A 3 The LORD has made known his victory; * his righteousness has he openly shown in the sight of the nations.

B 4 He remembers his mercy and faithfulness to the house of Israel, * and all the ends of the earth have seen the victory of our God. [ANT.]

A 5 Shout with joy to the LORD, all you lands; * lift up your voice, rejoice, and sing.

A 6 Sing to the LORD with the harp, * with the harp and the voice of song.

B 7 With trumpets and the sound of the horn * shout with joy before the King, the LORD. [ANT.]

A 8 Let the sea make a noise and all that is in it, * the lands and those who dwell therein.

A 9 Let the rivers clap their hands, * and let the hills ring out with joy before the LORD, when he comes to judge the earth.

B 10 In righteousness shall he judge the world * and the peoples with equity. [ANT.]

RCL Christmas 1 ABC Psalm 147: 13–21

based on "Divinum mysterium" (H82–82)

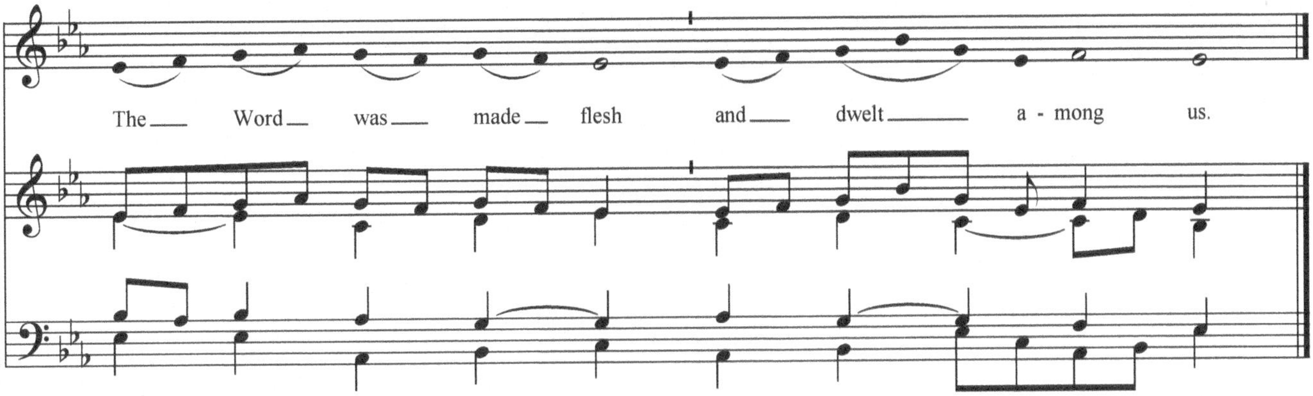

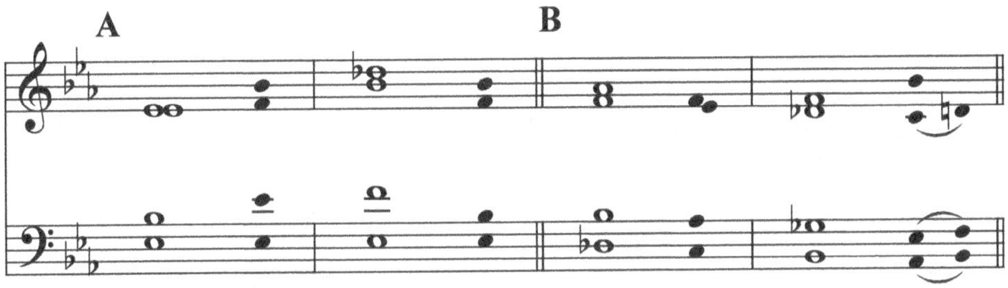

13 Worship the Lord, O Jerusalem; *
  praise your God, O Zion;
14 For he has strengthened the bars of your gates; *
  he has blessed your children within you. [ANT.]

15 He has established peace on your borders; *
  he satisfies you with the finest wheat.
16 He sends out his command to the earth, *
  and his word runs very swiftly. [ANT.]

A 17 He gives snow like wool; *
  he scatters hoarfrost like ashes.
A 18 He scatters his hail like bread crumbs; *
  who can stand against his cold?
B 19 He sends forth his word and melts them; *
  he blows with his wind, and the waters flow. [ANT.]

20 He declares his word to Jacob, *
  his statutes and his judgments to Israel.
21 He has not done so to any other nation; *
  to them he has not revealed his judgments.
  Hallelujah! [ANT.]

RCL Holy Name ABC Psalm 8

based on "Leoni" (H82–401)

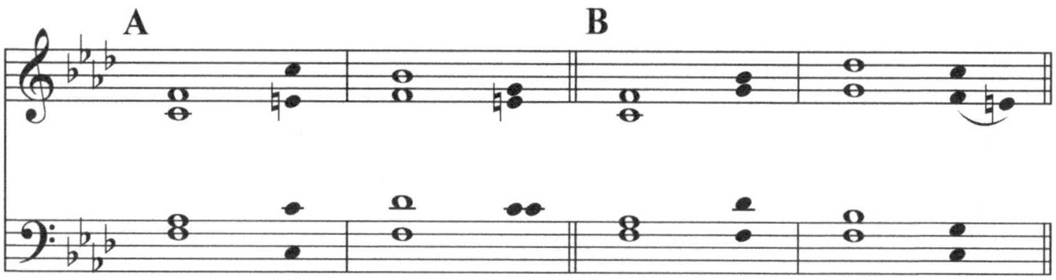

2 Out of the mouths of infants and children *
your majesty is praised above the heavens.
3 You have set up a stronghold against your adversaries, *
to quell the enemy and the avenger. [ANT.]

4 When I consider your heavens, the work of your fingers, *
the moon and the stars you have set in their courses,
5 What is man that you should be mindful of him? *
the son of man that you should seek him out? [ANT.]

A 6 You have made him but little lower than the angels; *
you adorn him with glory and honor;
B 7 You give him mastery over the works of your hands; *
you put all things under his feet:
A 8 All sheep and oxen, *
even the wild beasts of the field,
B 9 The birds of the air, the fish of the sea, *
and whatsoever walks in the paths of the sea. [ANT.]

RCL Christmas 2 ABC **Psalm 84: 1–8**

based on "Brother James' Air" (H82–517)

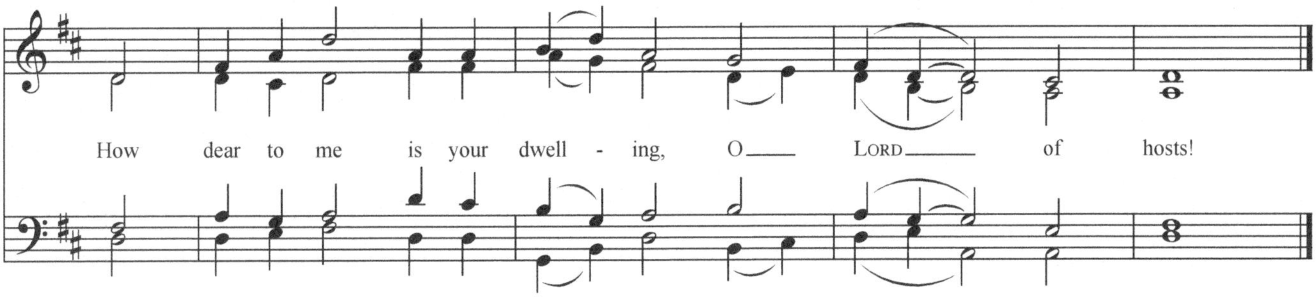

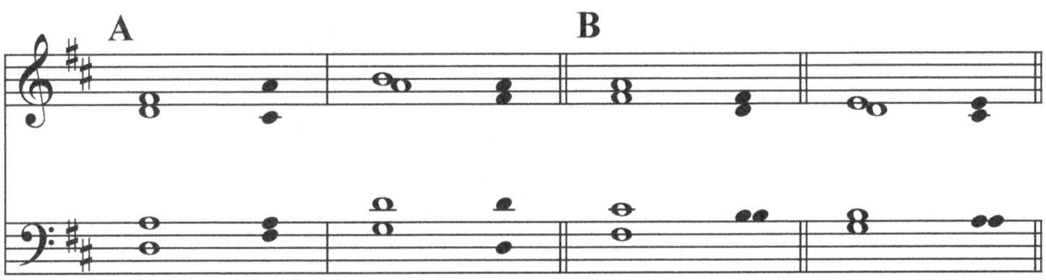

1b My soul has a desire and longing for the courts of
the LORD;
my heart and my flesh rejoice in the living God.
2 The sparrow has found her a house
and the swallow a nest where she may lay her young; *
by the side of your altars, O LORD of hosts,
my King and my God. [ANT.]

3 Happy are they who dwell in your house! *
they will always be praising you.
4 Happy are the people whose strength is in you! *
whose hearts are set on the pilgrims' way. [ANT.]

5 Those who go through the desolate valley will find
it a place of springs, *
for the early rains have covered it with pools of water.
6 They will climb from height to height, *
and the God of gods will reveal himself in Zion. [ANT.]

7 LORD God of hosts, hear my prayer; *
hearken, O God of Jacob.
8 Behold our defender, O God; *
and look upon the face of your Anointed. [ANT.]

RCL Epiphany ABC **Psalm 72: 1–7, 10–14**

based on "Es flog ein kleins Waldvögelein" (H82–616)

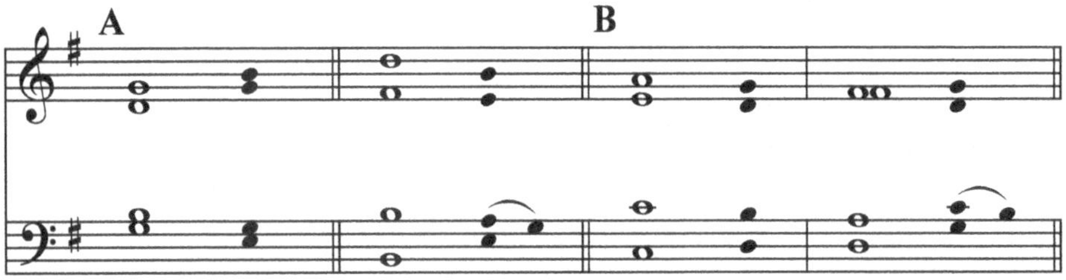

A 1 Give the King your justice, O God, *
and your righteousness to the King's Son;
A 2 That he may rule your people righteously *
and the poor with justice;
B 3 That the mountains may bring prosperity to the people, *
and the little hills bring righteousness. [ANT.]

A 4 He shall defend the needy among the people; *
he shall rescue the poor and crush the oppressor.
B 5 He shall live as long as the sun and moon endure, *
from one generation to another.
A 6 He shall come down like rain upon the mown field, *
like showers that water the earth.
B 7 In his time shall the righteous flourish; *
there shall be abundance of peace till the moon shall
be no more. [ANT.]

10 The kings of Tarshish and of the isles shall pay tribute, *
and the kings of Arabia and Saba offer gifts.
11 All kings shall bow down before him, *
and all the nations do him service. [ANT.]

A 12 For he shall deliver the poor who cries out in distress, *
and the oppressed who has no helper.
A 13 He shall have pity on the lowly and poor; *
he shall preserve the lives of the needy.
B 14 He shall redeem their lives from oppression and violence, *
and dear shall their blood be in his sight. [ANT.]

RCL Epiphany 1 ABC Psalm 29

based on "Deus tuorum militum" (H82–448)

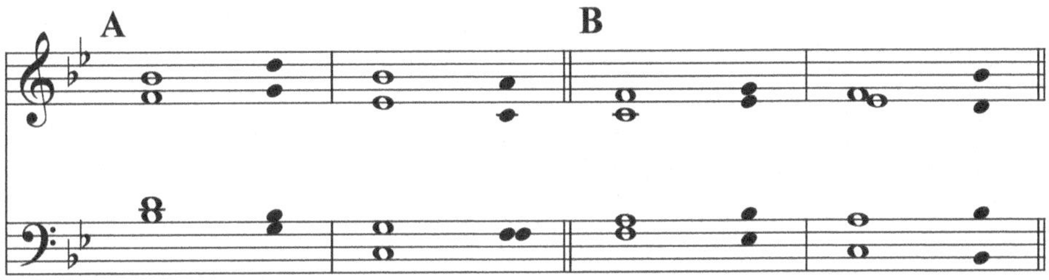

1 Ascribe to the Lord, you gods, *
ascribe to the Lord glory and strength.
2 Ascribe to the Lord the glory due his Name; *
worship the Lord in the beauty of holiness. [ANT.]

A 3 The voice of the Lord is upon the waters;
the God of glory thunders; *
the Lord is upon the mighty waters.
A 4 The voice of the Lord is a powerful voice; *
the voice of the Lord is a voice of splendor.
B 5 The voice of the Lord breaks the cedar trees; *
the Lord breaks the cedars of Lebanon; [ANT.]

6 He makes Lebanon skip like a calf, *
and Mount Hermon like a young wild ox.
7 The voice of the Lord splits the flames of fire;
the voice of the Lord shakes the wilderness; *
the Lord shakes the wilderness of Kadesh. [ANT.]

8 The voice of the Lord makes the oak trees writhe *
and strips the forests bare.
9 And in the temple of the Lord *
all are crying, "Glory!" [ANT.]

10 The Lord sits enthroned above the flood; *
the Lord sits enthroned as King for evermore.
11 The Lord shall give strength to his people; *
the Lord shall give his people the blessing of peace. [ANT.]

RCL Presentation ABC Psalm 84

based on "Brother James' Air" (H82–517)

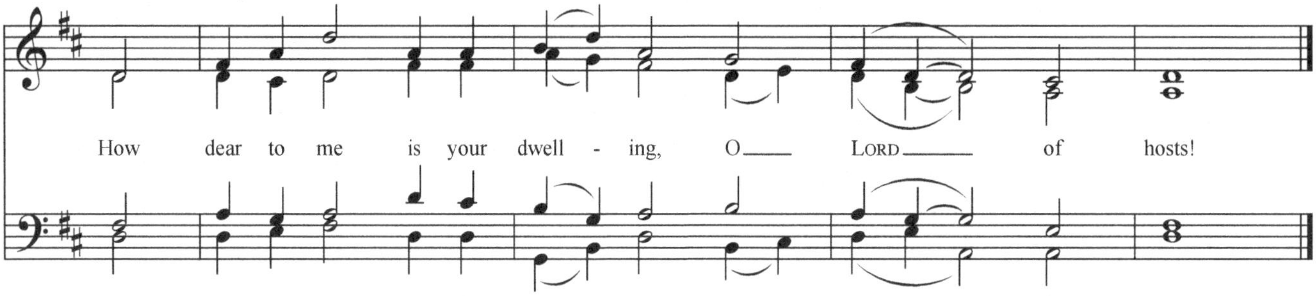

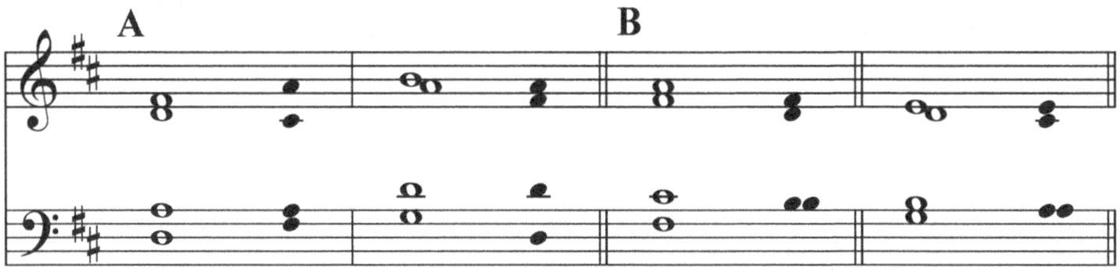

1b My soul has a desire and longing for the courts of
the Lord;
my heart and my flesh rejoice in the living God.
2 The sparrow has found her a house
and the swallow a nest where she may lay her young; *
by the side of your altars, O Lord of hosts,
my King and my God. [ANT.]

3 Happy are they who dwell in your house! *
they will always be praising you.
4 Happy are the people whose strength is in you! *
whose hearts are set on the pilgrims' way. [ANT.]

5 Those who go through the desolate valley will find
it a place of springs, *
for the early rains have covered it with pools of water.
6 They will climb from height to height, *
and the God of gods will reveal himself in Zion. [ANT.]

A 7 Lord God of hosts, hear my prayer; *
hearken, O God of Jacob.
A 8 Behold our defender, O God; *
and look upon the face of your Anointed.
B 9 For one day in your courts is better than
a thousand in my own room, *
and to stand at the threshold of the house of my God
than to dwell in the tents of the wicked. [ANT.]

A 10 For the Lord God is both sun and shield; *
he will give grace and glory;
A 11 No good thing will the Lord withhold *
from those who walk with integrity.
B 12 O Lord of hosts, *
happy are they who put their trust in you! [ANT.]

RCL Presentation ABC   Psalm 24:7–10

based on "Truro" (H82–436)

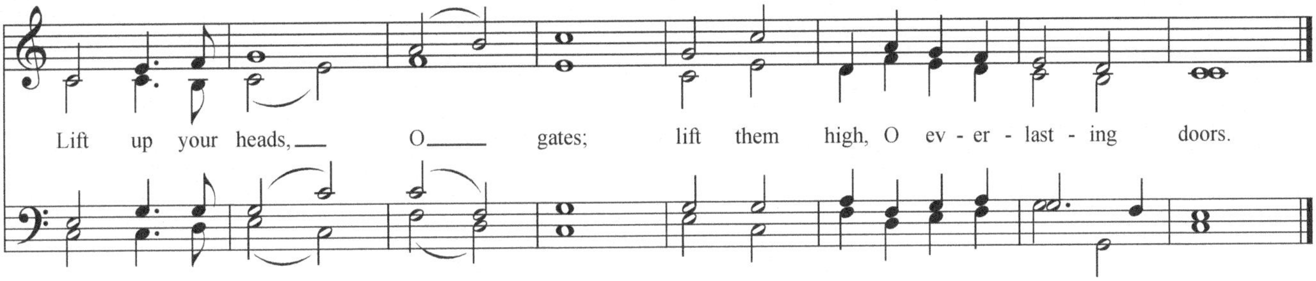

7 Lift up your heads, O gates;
lift them high, O everlasting doors; *
and the King of glory shall come in.
8 "Who is this King of glory?" *
"The LORD, strong and mighty,
the LORD, mighty in battle." [ANT.]

9 Lift up your heads, O gates;
lift them high, O everlasting doors; *
and the King of glory shall come in.
10 "Who is he, this King of glory?"
"The LORD of hosts,
he is the King of glory." [ANT.]

RCL Ash Wednesday ABC Psalm 103: 8–14

based on "Old 124th" (H82–149)

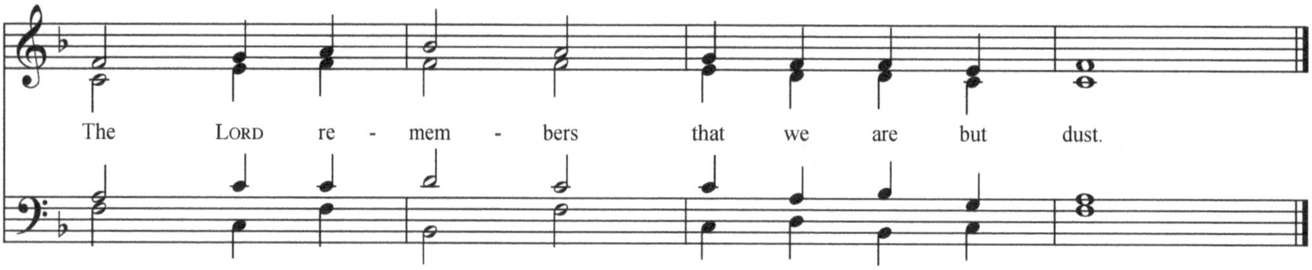

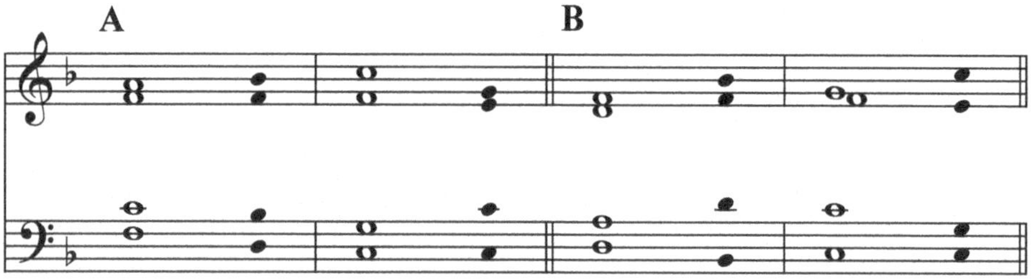

A 8 The LORD is full of compassion and mercy, *
slow to anger and of great kindness.
A 9 He will not always accuse us, *
nor will he keep his anger for ever.
B 10 He has not dealt with us according to our sins, *
nor rewarded us according to our wickedness. [ANT.]

11 For as the heavens are high above the earth, *
so is his mercy great upon those who fear him.
12 As far as the east is from the west, *
so far has he removed our sins from us. [ANT.]

13 As a father cares for his children, *
so does the LORD care for those who fear him.
14 For he himself knows whereof we are made; *
he remembers that we are but dust. [ANT.]

RCL Palm Sunday–Liturgy of the Palms ABC   Psalm 118: 1–2, 19–29

based on "Valet will ich dir geben" (H82–154)

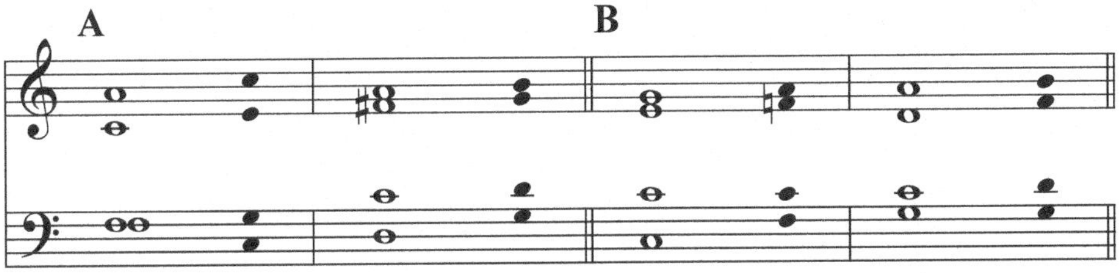

1 Give thanks to the LORD, for he is good; *
his mercy endures for ever.
2 Let Israel now proclaim, *
"His mercy endures for ever." [ANT.]

A 19 Open for me the gates of righteousness; *
I will enter them;
I will offer thanks to the LORD.
A 20 "This is the gate of the LORD; *
he who is righteous may enter."
B 21 I will give thanks to you, for you answered me *
and have become my salvation. [ANT.]

A 22 The same stone which the builders rejected *
has become the chief cornerstone.
A 23 This is the LORD's doing, *
and it is marvelous in our eyes.
B 24 On this day the LORD has acted; *
we will rejoice and be glad in it. [ANT.]

25 Hosannah, LORD, hosannah! *
LORD, send us now success.
26 Blessed is he who comes in the name of the LORD; *
we bless you from the house of the LORD. [ANT.]

A 27 God is the LORD; he has shined upon us; *
form a procession with branches
up to the horns of the altar.
A 28 "You are my God, and I will thank you; *
you are my God, and I will exalt you."
B 29 Give thanks to the LORD, for he is good; *
his mercy endures for ever. [ANT.]

RCL Palm Sunday ABC Psalm 31: 9–16

based on "Herzlich tut mich verlangen" (H82–168)

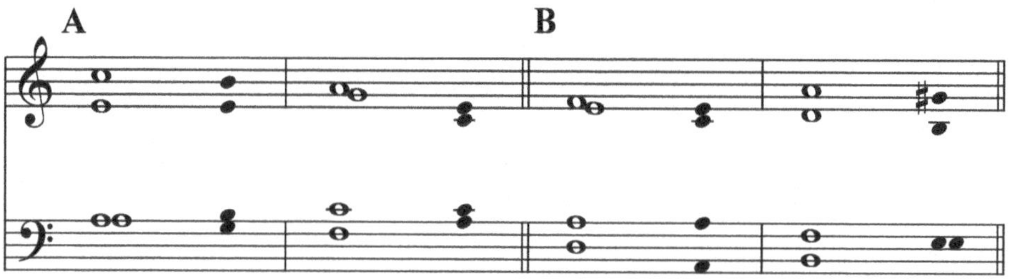

9 Have mercy on me, O LORD, for I am in trouble; *
my eye is consumed with sorrow,
and also my throat and my belly.
10 For my life is wasted with grief,
and my years with sighing; *
my strength fails me because of affliction,
and my bones are consumed. [ANT.]

11 I have become a reproach to all my enemies and even to my neighbors,
a dismay to those of my acquaintance; *
when they see me in the street they avoid me.
12 I am forgotten like a dead man, out of mind; *
I am as useless as a broken pot. [ANT.]

13 For I have heard the whispering of the crowd;
fear is all around; *
they put their heads together against me;
they plot to take my life.
14 But as for me, I have trusted in you, O LORD. *
I have said, "You are my God. [ANT.]

15 My times are in your hand; *
rescue me from the hand of my enemies,
and from those who persecute me.
16 Make your face to shine upon your servant, *
and in your loving-kindness save me." [ANT.]

RCL Monday in Holy Week ABC Psalm 36: 5–11

based on "Tender Thought" (H82–702)

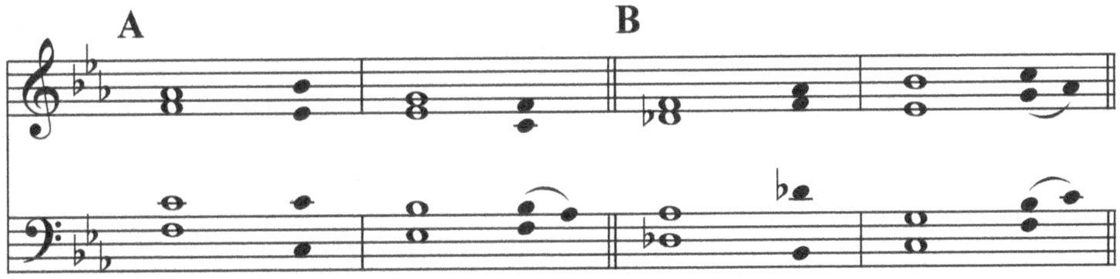

5 Your love, O LORD, reaches to the heavens, *
and your faithfulness to the clouds.
6 Your righteousness is like the strong mountains,
your justice like the great deep; *
you save both man and beast, O LORD. [ANT.]

7 How priceless is your love, O God! *
your people take refuge under the
shadow of your wings.
8 They feast upon the abundance of your house; *
you give them drink from the river of your delights. [ANT.]

A 9 For with you is the well of life, *
and in your light we see light.
A 10 Continue your loving-kindness to those who know you, *
and your favor to those who are true of heart. [ANT.]

B 11 Let not the foot of the proud come near me, *
nor the hand of the wicked push me aside. [ANT.]

RCL Tuesday in Holy Week ABC   Psalm 71: 1–14

based on "Slane" (H82–488)

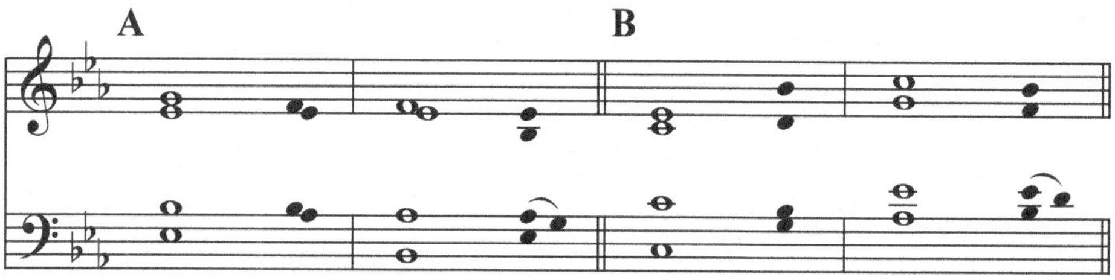

1 In you, O LORD, have I taken refuge; *
  let me never be ashamed.
2 In your righteousness, deliver me and set me free; *
  incline your ear to me and save me. [ANT.]

3 Be my strong rock, a castle to keep me safe; *
  you are my crag and my stronghold.
4 Deliver me, my God, from the hand of the wicked, *
  from the clutches of the evildoer and the oppressor. [ANT.]

A 5 For you are my hope, O Lord GOD, *
  my confidence since I was young.
B 6 I have been sustained by you ever since I was born;
from my mother's womb you have been my strength; *
  my praise shall be always of you.
A 7 I have become a portent to many; *
  but you are my refuge and my strength.
B 8 Let my mouth be full of your praise *
  and your glory all the day long. [ANT.]

A 9 Do not cast me off in my old age; *
  forsake me not when my strength fails.
A 10 For my enemies are talking against me, *
  and those who lie in wait for my life take counsel together.
B 11 They say, "God has forsaken him;
go after him and seize him; *
  because there is none who will save." [ANT.]

A 12 O God, be not far from me; *
  come quickly to help me, O my God.
A 13 Let those who set themselves against me
be put to shame and be disgraced; *
  let those who seek to do me evil be
  covered with scorn and reproach.
B 14 But I shall always wait in patience, *
  and shall praise you more and more. [ANT.]

RCL Wednesday in Holy Week ABC Psalm 70

based on "Balm in Gilead" (H82–676)

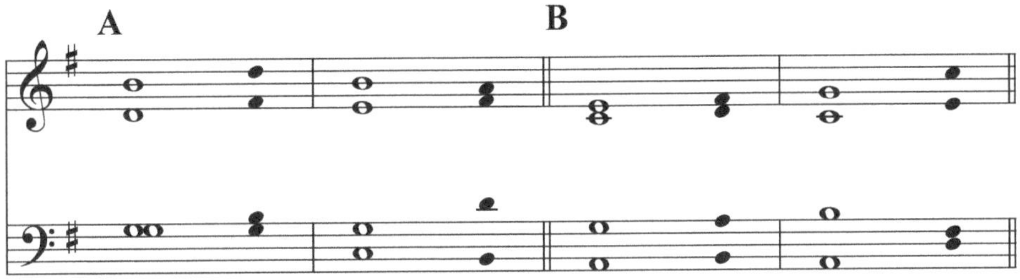

1 Be pleased, O God, to deliver me; *
O LORD, make haste to help me.
2 Let those who seek my life be ashamed
and altogether dismayed; *
let those who take pleasure in my misfortune
draw back and be disgraced. [ANT.]

3 Let those who say to me "Aha!" and gloat over me turn back, *
because they are ashamed.
4 Let all who seek you rejoice and be glad in you; *
let those who love your salvation say for ever,
"Great is the LORD!" [ANT.]

5 But as for me, I am poor and needy; *
come to me speedily, O God.
6 You are my helper and my deliverer; *
O LORD, do not tarry. [ANT.]

RCL Maundy Thursday ABC **Psalm 116: 1, 10–17**

based on "Let Us Break Bread Together" (H82–325)

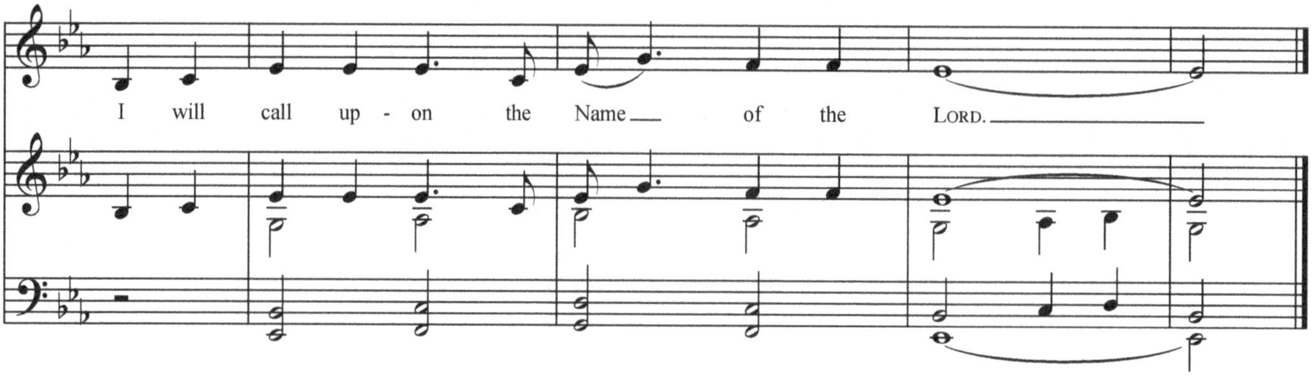

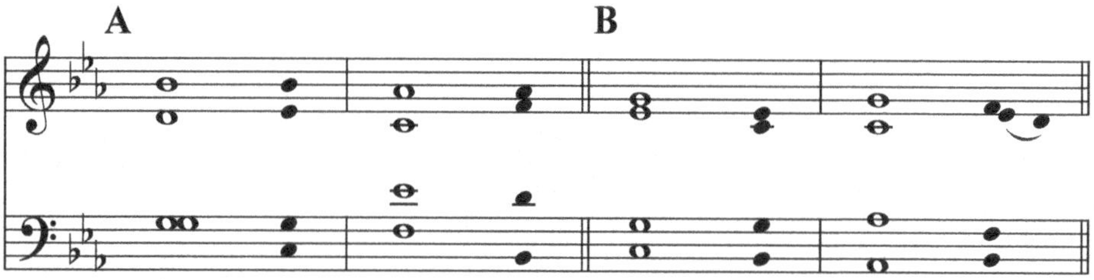

	1	I love the LORD, because he has heard the voice of my supplication, * because he has inclined his ear to me whenever I called upon him. [ANT.]
A	10	How shall I repay the LORD * for all the good things he has done for me?
A	11	I will lift up the cup of salvation * and call upon the Name of the LORD.
B	12	I will fulfill my vows to the LORD * in the presence of all his people. [ANT.]
	13	Precious in the sight of the LORD * is the death of his servants.
	14	O LORD, I am your servant; * I am your servant and the child of your handmaid; you have freed me from my bonds. [ANT.]
A	15	I will offer you the sacrifice of thanksgiving * and call upon the Name of the LORD.
A	16	I will fulfill my vows to the LORD * in the presence of all his people,
B	17	In the courts of the LORD's house, * in the midst of you, O Jerusalem. [ANT.]

This page intentionally left blank

RCL Good Friday ABC Psalm 22

based on "Bangor" (H82–164)

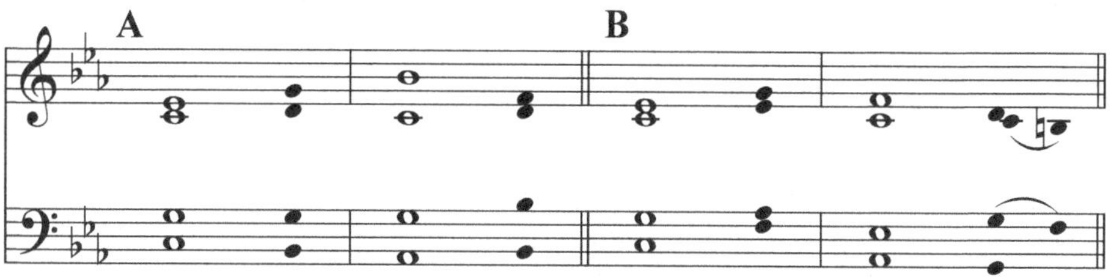

1 My God, my God, why have you forsaken me? *
  and are so far from my cry
  and from the words of my distress?
2 O my God, I cry in the daytime, but you do not answer; *
  by night as well, but I find no rest. [ANT.]

A 3 Yet you are the Holy One, *
  enthroned upon the praises of Israel.
A 4 Our forefathers put their trust in you; *
  they trusted, and you delivered them.
B 5 They cried out to you and were delivered; *
  they trusted in you and were not put to shame. [ANT.]

A 6 But as for me, I am a worm and no man, *
  scorned by all and despised by the people.
A 7 All who see me laugh me to scorn; *
  they curl their lips and wag their heads, saying,
B 8 "He trusted in the LORD; let him deliver him; *
  let him rescue him, if he delights in him." [ANT.]

A 9 Yet you are he who took me out of the womb, *
  and kept me safe upon my mother's breast.
A 10 I have been entrusted to you ever since I was born; *
  you were my God when I was still in my
    mother's womb.
B 11 Be not far from me, for trouble is near, *
  and there is none to help. [ANT.]

A 12 Many young bulls encircle me; *
strong bulls of Bashan surround me.
B 13 They open wide their jaws at me, *
like a ravening and a roaring lion.
A 14 I am poured out like water;
all my bones are out of joint; *
my heart within my breast is melting wax.
B 15 My mouth is dried out like a pot-sherd;
my tongue sticks to the roof of my mouth; *
and you have laid me in the dust of the grave. [ANT.]

16 Packs of dogs close me in,
and gangs of evildoers circle around me; *
they pierce my hands and my feet;
I can count all my bones.
17 They stare and gloat over me; *
they divide my garments among them;
they cast lots for my clothing. [ANT.]

A 18 Be not far away, O LORD; *
you are my strength; hasten to help me.
B 19 Save me from the sword, *
my life from the power of the dog.
A 20 Save me from the lion's mouth, *
my wretched body from the horns of wild bulls.
B 21 I will declare your Name to my brethren; *
in the midst of the congregation I will praise you. [ANT.]

A 22 Praise the LORD, you that fear him; *
stand in awe of him, O offspring of Israel;
all you of Jacob's line, give glory.
A 23 For he does not despise nor abhor the poor in their poverty;
neither does he hide his face from them; *
but when they cry to him he hears them.
B 24 My praise is of him in the great assembly; *
I will perform my vows in the presence of those who
worship him. [ANT.]

A 25 The poor shall eat and be satisfied,
and those who seek the LORD shall praise him: *
"May your heart live for ever!"
B 26 All the ends of the earth shall remember and turn to
the LORD, *
and all the families of the nations shall bow before him.
A 27 For kingship belongs to the LORD; *
he rules over the nations.
B 28 To him alone all who sleep in the earth bow down
in worship; *
all who go down to the dust fall before him. [ANT.]

29 My soul shall live for him;
my descendants shall serve him; *
they shall be known as the LORD's for ever.
30 They shall come and make known to a people yet unborn *
the saving deeds that he has done. [ANT.]

RCL Holy Saturday ABC Psalm 31: 1–4, 15–16

based on "Pleading Savior" (H82–586)

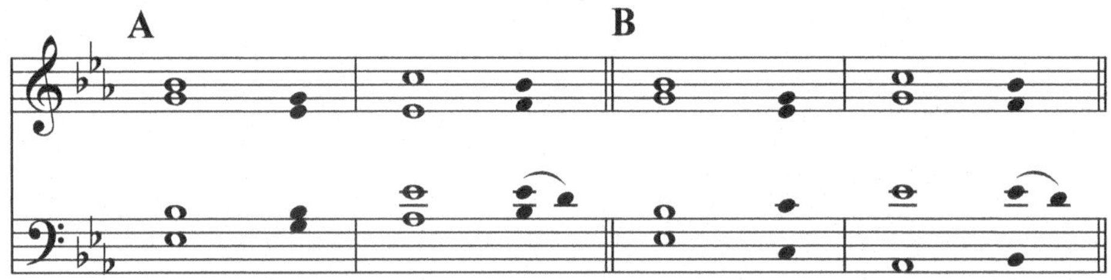

1 In you, O LORD, have I taken refuge;
let me never be put to shame: *
deliver me in your righteousness.
2 Incline your ear to me; *
make haste to deliver me. [ANT.]

3 Be my strong rock, a castle to keep me safe,
for you are my crag and my stronghold; *
for the sake of your Name, lead me and guide me.
4 Take me out of the net that they have secretly set for me, *
for you are my tower of strength. [ANT.]

15 My times are in your hand; *
rescue me from the hand of my enemies,
and from those who persecute me.
16 Make your face to shine upon your servant, *
and in your loving-kindness save me. [ANT.]

RCL Great Vigil of Easter ABC Psalm 136: 1–9, 23–26

based on "Wareham" (H82–137)

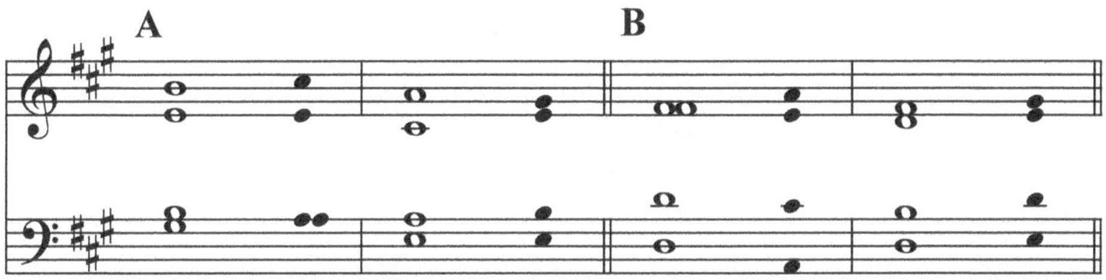

A 1 Give thanks to the LORD, for he is good, *
for his mercy endures for ever.
A 2 Give thanks to the God of gods, *
for his mercy endures for ever.
B 3 Give thanks to the Lord of lords, *
for his mercy endures for ever. [ANT.]

A 4 Who only does great wonders, *
for his mercy endures for ever;
A 5 Who by wisdom made the heavens, *
for his mercy endures for ever;
B 6 Who spread out the earth upon the waters, *
for his mercy endures for ever; [ANT.]

A 7 Who created great lights, *
for his mercy endures for ever;
A 8 The sun to rule the day, *
for his mercy endures for ever;
B 9 The moon and the stars to govern the night, *
for his mercy endures for ever. [ANT.]

23 Who remembered us in our low estate, *
for his mercy endures for ever;
24 And delivered us from our enemies, *
for his mercy endures for ever; [ANT.]

25 Who gives food to all creatures, *
for his mercy endures for ever.
26 Give thanks to the God of heaven, *
for his mercy endures for ever. [ANT.]

RCL Great Vigil of Easter ABC Psalm 46

based on "Ein feste burg" (H82–688)

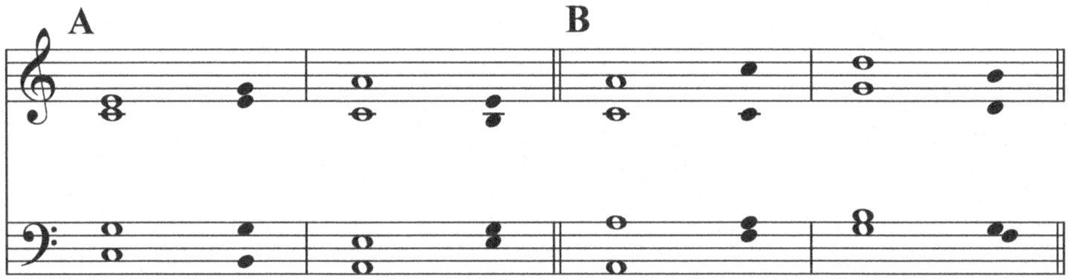

A 1 God is our refuge and strength, *
a very present help in trouble.
A 2 Therefore we will not fear, though the earth be moved, *
and though the mountains be toppled into the
depths of the sea;
B 3 Though its waters rage and foam, *
and though the mountains tremble at its tumult. [ANT.]

A 5 There is a river whose streams make glad the city of God, *
the holy habitation of the Most High.
A 6 God is in the midst of her;
she shall not be overthrown; *
God shall help her at the break of day.
B 7 The nations make much ado, and the kingdoms are shaken; *
God has spoken, and the earth shall melt away. [ANT.]

A 9 Come now and look upon the works of the LORD, *
what awesome things he has done on earth.
A 10 It is he who makes war to cease in all the world; *
he breaks the bow, and shatters the spear,
and burns the shields with fire.
B 11 "Be still, then, and know that I am God; *
I will be exalted among the nations;
I will be exalted in the earth." [ANT.]

RCL Great Vigil of Easter ABC Psalm 16

based on "Toplady" (H82–685)

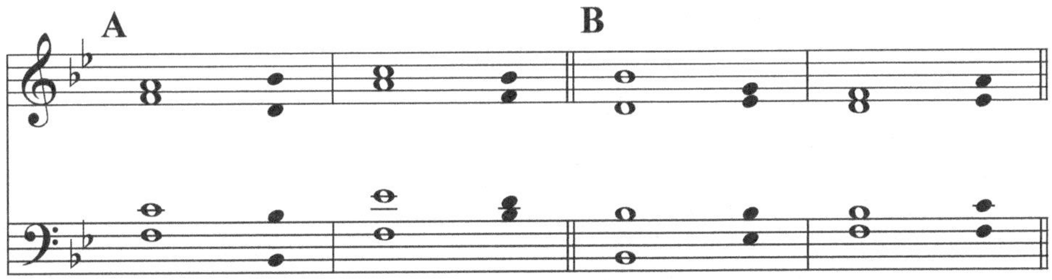

1b I have said to the LORD, "You are my Lord,
my good above all other."
2 All my delight is upon the godly that are in the land, *
upon those who are noble among the people. [ANT.]

3 But those who run after other gods *
shall have their troubles multiplied.
4 Their libations of blood I will not offer, *
nor take the names of their gods upon my lips. [ANT.]

5 O LORD, you are my portion and my cup; *
it is you who uphold my lot.
6 My boundaries enclose a pleasant land; *
indeed, I have a goodly heritage. [ANT.]

7 I will bless the LORD who gives me counsel; *
my heart teaches me, night after night.
8 I have set the LORD always before me; *
because he is at my right hand I shall not fall. [ANT.]

A 9 My heart, therefore, is glad, and my spirit rejoices; *
my body also shall rest in hope.
A 10 For you will not abandon me to the grave, *
nor let your holy one see the Pit.
B 11 You will show me the path of life; *
in your presence there is fullness of joy,
and in your right hand are pleasures for evermore. [ANT.]

RCL Great Vigil of Easter ABC   Canticle 8

based on "Old 100th" (H82–377)

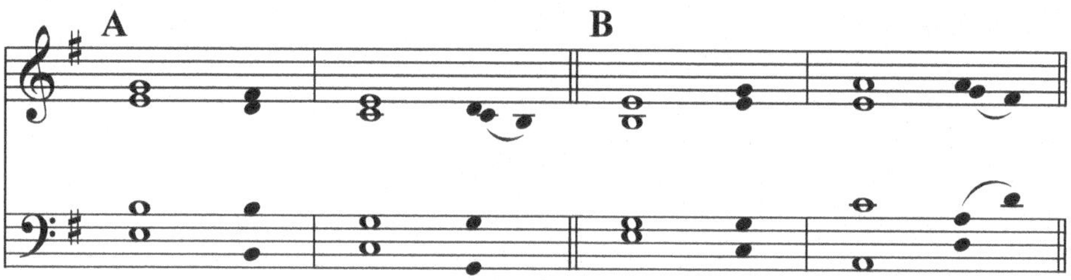

1 I will sing to the Lord, for he is lofty and uplifted; *
the horse and its rider has he hurled into the sea.
2 The Lord is my strength and my refuge; *
the Lord has become my Savior. [ANT.]

3 This is my God and I will praise him, *
the God of my people and I will exalt him.
4 The Lord is a mighty warrior; *
Yahweh is his Name. [ANT.]

5 The chariots of Pharaoh and his army has he hurled into the sea; *
the finest of those who bear armor have been
drowned in the Red Sea.
6 The fathomless deep has overwhelmed them; *
they sank into the depths like a stone. [ANT.]

A 7 Your right hand, O Lord, is glorious in might; *
your right hand, O Lord, has overthrown the enemy.
A 8 Who can be compared with you, O Lord, among the gods? *
who is like you, glorious in holiness,
awesome in renown, and worker of wonders?
B 9 You stretched forth your right hand; *
the earth swallowed them up. [ANT.]

A 10 With your constant love you led the people you redeemed; *
with your might you brought them in safety to
your holy dwelling.
B 11 You will bring them in and plant them *
on the mount of your possession,
A 12 The resting-place you have made for yourself, O Lord, *
the sanctuary, O Lord, that your hand has established.
B 13 The Lord shall reign *
for ever and for ever. [ANT.]

RCL Great Vigil of Easter ABC   Canticle 9

based on "Bunessan" (H82–8)

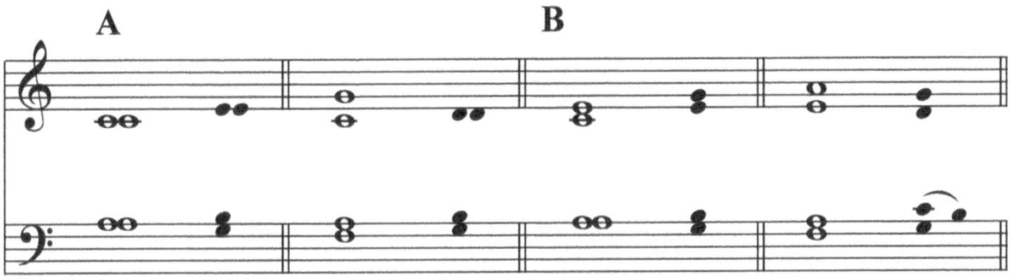

1 Surely, it is God who saves me; *
   I will trust in him and not be afraid.
2 For the Lord is my stronghold and my sure defense, *
   and he will be my Savior. [ANT.]

4 And on that day you shall say, *
   Give thanks to the Lord and call upon his Name;
5 Make his deeds known among the peoples; *
   see that they remember that his Name is exalted. [ANT.]

6 Sing the praises of the Lord, for he has done great things, *
   and this is known in all the world.
7 Cry aloud, inhabitants of Zion, ring out your joy, *
   for the great one in the midst of you is the Holy One of Israel. [ANT.]

RCL Great Vigil of Easter ABC   Psalm 19

based on "Song 1" (H82–499)

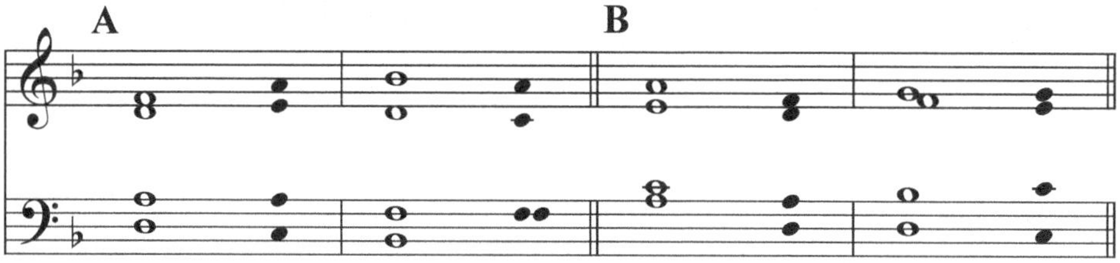

A 1 The heavens declare the glory of God, *
and the firmament shows his handiwork.
B 2 One day tells its tale to another, *
and one night imparts knowledge to another.
A 3 Although they have no words or language, *
and their voices are not heard,
B 4 Their sound has gone out into all lands, *
and their message to the ends of the world. [ANT.]

5 In the deep has he set a pavilion for the sun; *
it comes forth like a bridegroom out of his chamber;
it rejoices like a champion to run its course.
6 It goes forth from the uttermost edge of the heavens
and runs about to the end of it again; *
nothing is hidden from its burning heat. [ANT.]

7 The law of the LORD is perfect
and revives the soul; *
the testimony of the LORD is sure
and gives wisdom to the innocent.
8 The statutes of the LORD are just
and rejoice the heart; *
the commandment of the LORD is clear
and gives light to the eyes. [ANT.]

9 The fear of the LORD is clean
and endures for ever; *
the judgments of the LORD are true
and righteous altogether.
10 More to be desired are they than gold,
more than much fine gold, *
sweeter far than honey,
than honey in the comb. [ANT.]

11 By them also is your servant enlightened, *
and in keeping them there is great reward.
12 Who can tell how often he offends? *
cleanse me from my secret faults. [ANT.]

13 Above all, keep your servant from presumptuous sins;
let them not get dominion over me; *
then shall I be whole and sound,
and innocent of a great offense.
14 Let the words of my mouth and the meditation of my
heart be acceptable in your sight, *
O LORD, my strength and my redeemer. [ANT.]

This page intentionally left blank

RCL Great Vigil of Easter ABC   Psalms 42 & 43

based on "Wondrous Love" (H82–439)

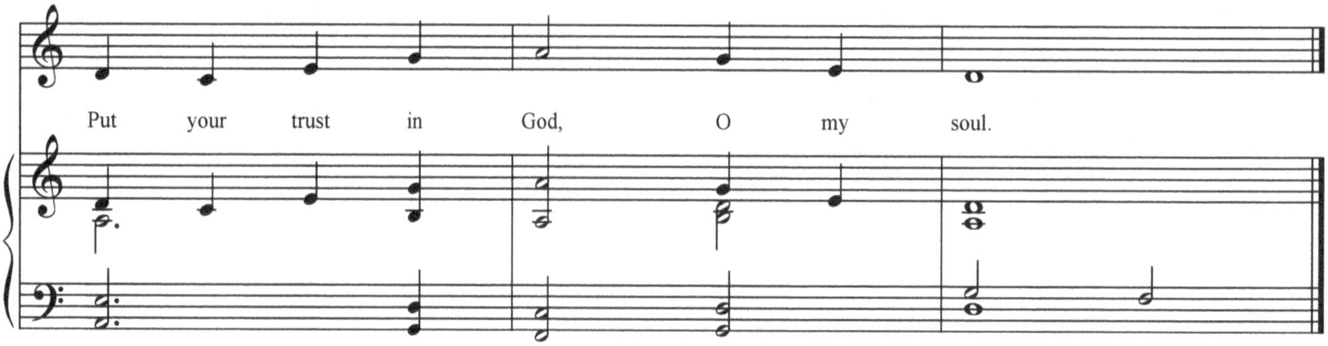

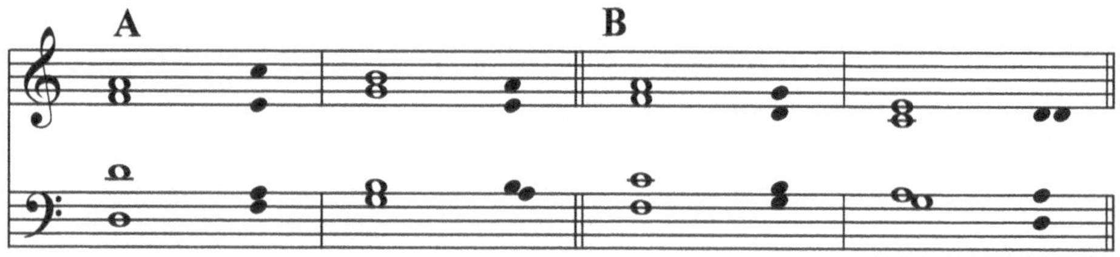

A 1 As the deer longs for the water-brooks, *
so longs my soul for you, O God.
A 2 My soul is athirst for God, athirst for the living God; *
when shall I come to appear before the presence of God?
B 3 My tears have been my food day and night, *
while all day long they say to me,
"Where now is your God?" [ANT.]

A 4 I pour out my soul when I think on these things: *
how I went with the multitude and led them into the
house of God,
B 5 With the voice of praise and thanksgiving, *
among those who keep holy-day. [ANT.]

A 6 Why are you so full of heaviness, O my soul? *
and why are you so disquieted within me?
B 7 Put your trust in God; *
for I will yet give thanks to him,
who is the help of my countenance, and my God. [ANT.]

A 8 My soul is heavy within me; *
therefore I will remember you from the land of Jordan,
and from the peak of Mizar among the heights of Hermon.
A 9 One deep calls to another in the noise of your cataracts; *
all your rapids and floods have gone over me.
B 10 The LORD grants his loving-kindness in the daytime; *
in the night season his song is with me,
a prayer to the God of my life. [ANT.]

A 11 I will say to the God of my strength,
"Why have you forgotten me? *
and why do I go so heavily while the enemy
oppresses me?"
A 12 While my bones are being broken, *
my enemies mock me to my face;
B 13 All day long they mock me *
and say to me, "Where now is your God?" [ANT.]

14 Why are you so full of heaviness, O my soul? *
and why are you so disquieted within me?
15 Put your trust in God; *
for I will yet give thanks to him,
who is the help of my countenance, and my God. [ANT.]

1 Give judgment for me, O God,
and defend my cause against an ungodly people; *
deliver me from the deceitful and the wicked.
2 For you are the God of my strength;
why have you put me from you? *
and why do I go so heavily while the enemy
oppresses me? [ANT.]

3 Send out your light and your truth, that they may lead me, *
and bring me to your holy hill
and to your dwelling;
4 That I may go to the altar of God,
to the God of my joy and gladness; *
and on the harp I will give thanks to you,
O God my God. [ANT.]

5 Why are you so full of heaviness, O my soul? *
and why are you so disquieted within me?
6 Put your trust in God; *
for I will yet give thanks to him,
who is the help of my countenance, and my God. [ANT.]

RCL Great Vigil of Easter ABC Psalm 143

based on "Victimae Paschali laudes" (H82–183)

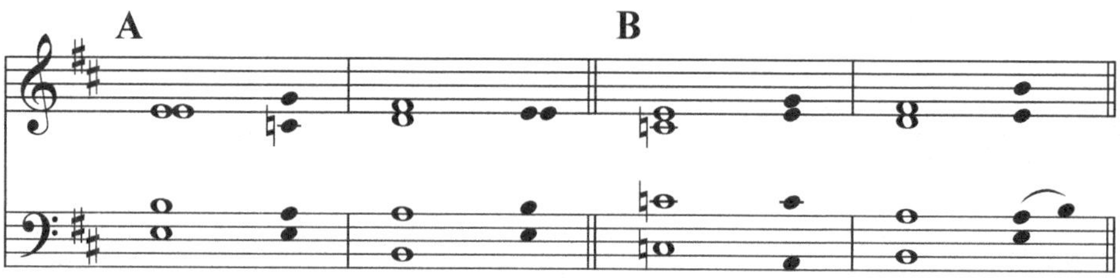

1 LORD, hear my prayer,
and in your faithfulness heed my supplications; *
answer me in your righteousness.
2 Enter not into judgment with your servant, *
for in your sight shall no one living be justified. [ANT.]

3 For my enemy has sought my life;
he has crushed me to the ground; *
he has made me live in dark places like those who are long dead.
4 My spirit faints within me; *
my heart within me is desolate. [ANT.]

5 I remember the time past;
I muse upon all your deeds; *
I consider the works of your hands.
6 I spread out my hands to you; *
my soul gasps to you like a thirsty land. [ANT.]

7 O LORD, make haste to answer me; my spirit fails me; *
do not hide your face from me
or I shall be like those who go down to the Pit.
8 Let me hear of your loving-kindness in the morning,
for I put my trust in you; *
show me the road that I must walk,
for I lift up my soul to you. [ANT.]

9 Deliver me from my enemies, O LORD, *
for I flee to you for refuge.
10 Teach me to do what pleases you,
for you are my God; *
let your good Spirit lead me
on level ground. [ANT.]

11 Revive me, O LORD, for your Name's sake; *
for your righteousness' sake,
bring me out of trouble.
12 Of your goodness, destroy my enemies
and bring all my foes to naught, *
for truly I am your servant. [ANT.]

RCL Great Vigil of Easter ABC Psalm 98

based on "Rendez à Dieu" (H82–301, 302, 413)

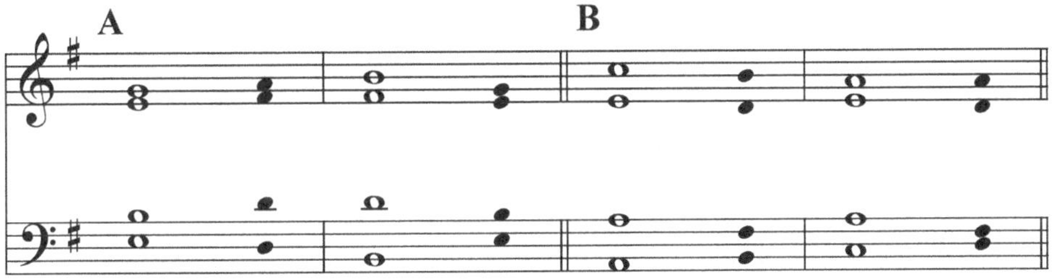

1 Sing to the LORD a new song, *
for he has done marvelous things.
2 With his right hand and his holy arm *
has he won for himself the victory. [ANT.]

3 The LORD has made known his victory; *
his righteousness has he openly shown in the sight of the nations.
4 He remembers his mercy and faithfulness to the house of Israel, *
and all the ends of the earth have seen the victory of our God. [ANT.]

A 5 Shout with joy to the LORD, all you lands; *
lift up your voice, rejoice, and sing.
A 6 Sing to the LORD with the harp, *
with the harp and the voice of song.
B 7 With trumpets and the sound of the horn *
shout with joy before the King, the LORD. [ANT.]

A 8 Let the sea make a noise and all that is in it, *
the lands and those who dwell therein.
A 9 Let the rivers clap their hands, *
and let the hills ring out with joy before the LORD,
when he comes to judge the earth.
B 10 In righteousness shall he judge the world *
and the peoples with equity. [ANT.]

RCL Easter Day (Early) ABC   Psalm 114

based on "O filii et filiae" (H82–206)

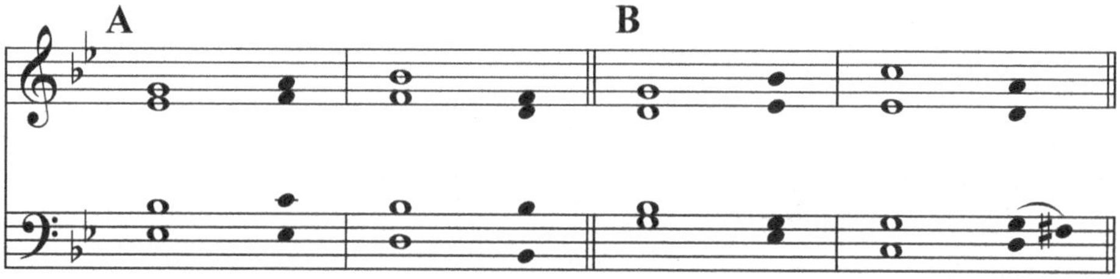

1 Hallelujah!
When Israel came out of Egypt, *
the house of Jacob from a people of strange speech,
2 Judah became God's sanctuary *
and Israel his dominion. [ANT.]

3 The sea beheld it and fled; *
Jordan turned and went back.
4 The mountains skipped like rams, *
and the little hills like young sheep. [ANT.]

5 What ailed you, O sea, that you fled? *
O Jordan, that you turned back?
6 You mountains, that you skipped like rams? *
you little hills like young sheep? [ANT.]

7 Tremble, O earth, at the presence of the LORD, *
at the presence of the God of Jacob,
8 Who turned the hard rock into a pool of water *
and flint-stone into a flowing spring. [ANT.]

RCL Easter Day ABC (Principal Service) **Psalm 118: 1–2, 14–24**

based on "Easter Hymn" (H82–207)

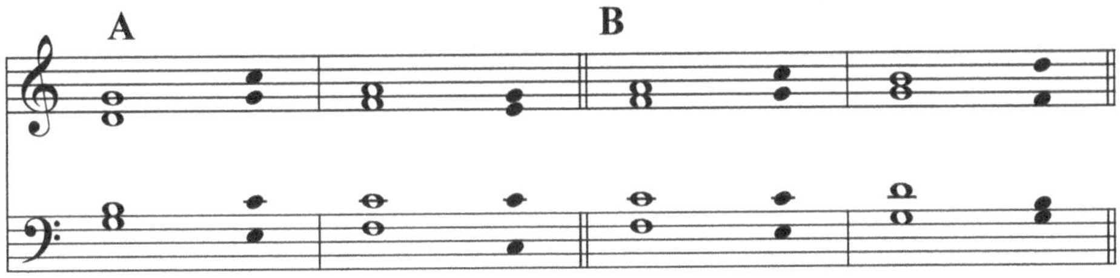

1 Give thanks to the LORD, for he is good; *
his mercy endures for ever.
2 Let Israel now proclaim, *
"His mercy endures for ever." [ANT.]

A 14 The LORD is my strength and my song, *
and he has become my salvation.
A 15 There is a sound of exultation and victory *
in the tents of the righteous:
B 16 "The right hand of the LORD has triumphed! *
the right hand of the LORD is exalted!
the right hand of the LORD has triumphed!" [ANT.]

17 I shall not die, but live, *
and declare the works of the LORD.
18 The Lord has punished me sorely, *
but he did not hand me over to death. [ANT.]

A 19 Open for me the gates of righteousness; *
I will enter them;
I will offer thanks to the LORD.
A 20 "This is the gate of the LORD; *
he who is righteous may enter."
B 21 I will give thanks to you, for you answered me *
and have become my salvation. [ANT.]

22 The same stone which the builders rejected *
has become the chief cornerstone.
23 This is the LORD's doing, *
and it is marvelous in our eyes. [ANT.]

RCL Easter Day (Evening) ABC Psalm 114

based on "O filii et filiae" (H82–206)

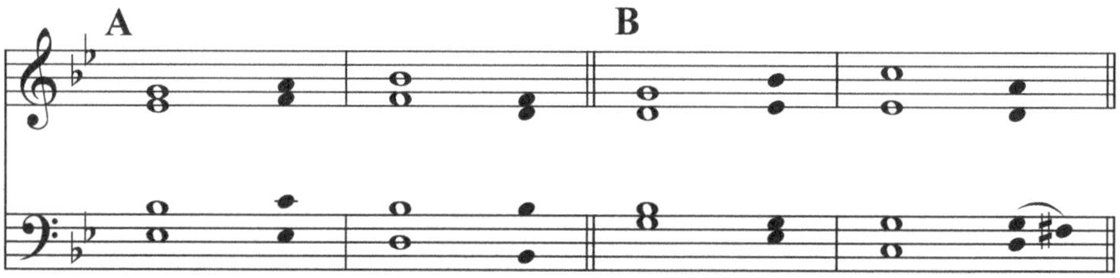

1 Hallelujah!
When Israel came out of Egypt, *
the house of Jacob from a people of strange speech,
2 Judah became God's sanctuary *
and Israel his dominion. [ANT.]

3 The sea beheld it and fled; *
Jordan turned and went back.
4 The mountains skipped like rams, *
and the little hills like young sheep. [ANT.]

5 What ailed you, O sea, that you fled? *
O Jordan, that you turned back?
6 You mountains, that you skipped like rams? *
you little hills like young sheep? [ANT.]

7 Tremble, O earth, at the presence of the Lord, *
at the presence of the God of Jacob,
8 Who turned the hard rock into a pool of water *
and flint-stone into a flowing spring. [ANT.]

RCL Monday in Easter Week ABC Psalm 16: 8–11

based on "O filii et filiae" (H82–206)

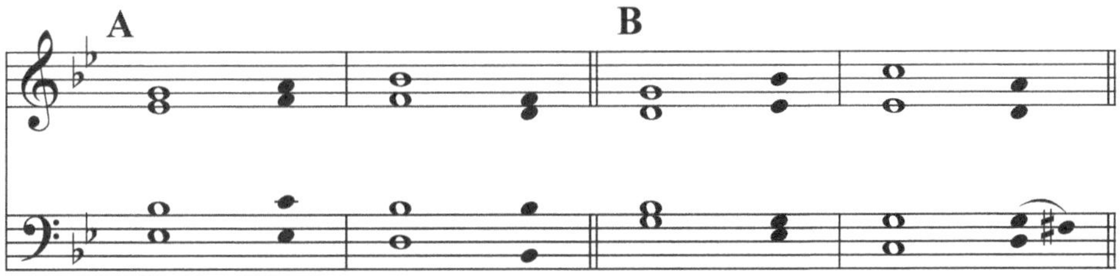

8 I have set the LORD always before me; *
because he is at my right hand I shall not fall.
9 My heart, therefore, is glad, and my spirit rejoices; *
my body also shall rest in hope. [ANT.]

10 For you will not abandon me to the grave, *
nor let your holy one see the Pit.
11 You will show me the path of life; *
in your presence there is fullness of joy,
and in your right hand are pleasures for evermore. [ANT.]

RCL Monday-Saturday in Easter Week ABC Psalm 118: 19–24

based on "O filii et filiae" (H82–206)

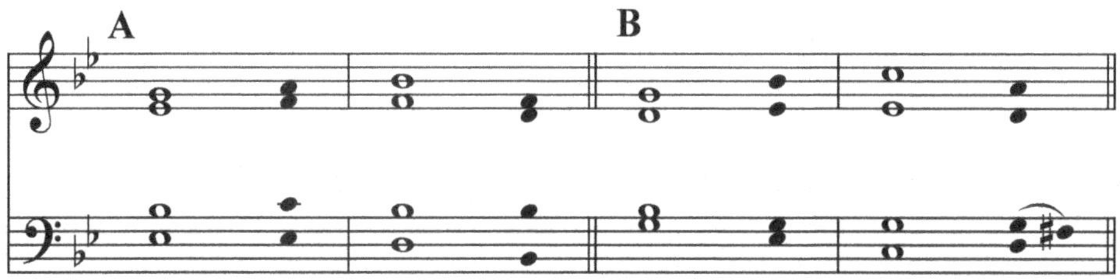

A 19 Open for me the gates of righteousness; *
I will enter them;
I will offer thanks to the LORD.

A 20 "This is the gate of the LORD; *
he who is righteous may enter."

B 21 I will give thanks to you, for you answered me *
and have become my salvation. [ANT.]

A 22 The same stone which the builders rejected *
has become the chief cornerstone.

A 23 This is the LORD's doing, *
and it is marvelous in our eyes.

B 24 On this day the LORD has acted; *
we will rejoice and be glad in it. [ANT.]

RCL Tuesday in Easter Week ABC Psalm 33: 18–22

based on "Gelobt sei Gott" (H82–205)

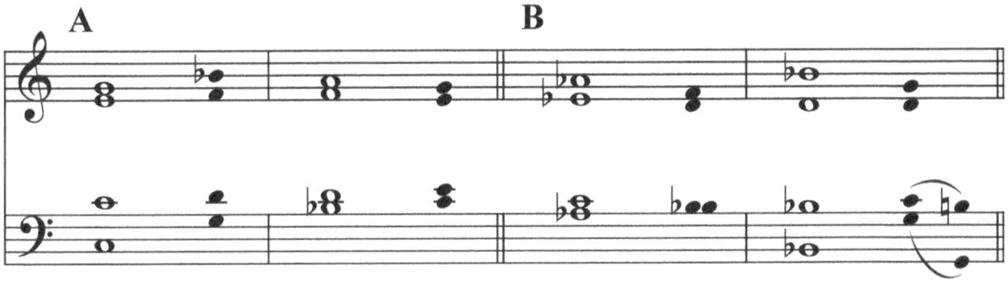

18 Behold, the eye of the Lord is upon those who fear him, *
on those who wait upon his love,
19 To pluck their lives from death, *
and to feed them in time of famine. [ANT.]

A 20 Our soul waits for the Lord; *
he is our help and our shield.
A 21 Indeed, our heart rejoices in him, *
for in his holy Name we put our trust.
B 22 Let your loving-kindness, O Lord, be upon us, *
as we have put our trust in you. [ANT.]

RCL Wednesday in Easter Week ABC Psalm 105: 1–8

based on "O filii et filiae" (H82–206)

1 Give thanks to the LORD and call upon his Name; *
make known his deeds among the peoples.
2 Sing to him, sing praises to him, *
and speak of all his marvelous works. [ANT.]

3 Glory in his holy Name; *
let the hearts of those who seek the Lord rejoice.
4 Search for the LORD and his strength; *
continually seek his face. [ANT.]

5 Remember the marvels he has done, *
his wonders and the judgments of his mouth,
6 O offspring of Abraham his servant, *
O children of Jacob his chosen. [ANT.]

7 He is the LORD our God; *
his judgments prevail in all the world.
8 He has always been mindful of his covenant, *
the promise he made for a thousand generations: [ANT.]

RCL Thursday in Easter Week ABC Psalm 8

based on "O filii et filiae" (H82–206)

A 1 O LORD our Governor, *
how exalted is your Name in all the world!
A 2 Out of the mouths of infants and children *
your majesty is praised above the heavens.
B 3 You have set up a stronghold against your adversaries, *
to quell the enemy and the avenger. [ANT.]

4 When I consider your heavens, the work of your fingers, *
the moon and the stars you have set in their courses,
5 What is man that you should be mindful of him? *
the son of man that you should seek him out? [ANT.]

6 You have made him but little lower than the angels; *
you adorn him with glory and honor;
7 You give him mastery over the works of your hands; *
you put all things under his feet: [ANT.]

A 8 All sheep and oxen, *
even the wild beasts of the field,
A 9 The birds of the air, the fish of the sea, *
and whatsoever walks in the paths of the sea.
B 10 O LORD our Governor, *
how exalted is your Name in all the world! [ANT.]

RCL Friday in Easter Week ABC **Psalm 116: 1–8**

based on "Victory" (H82–208)

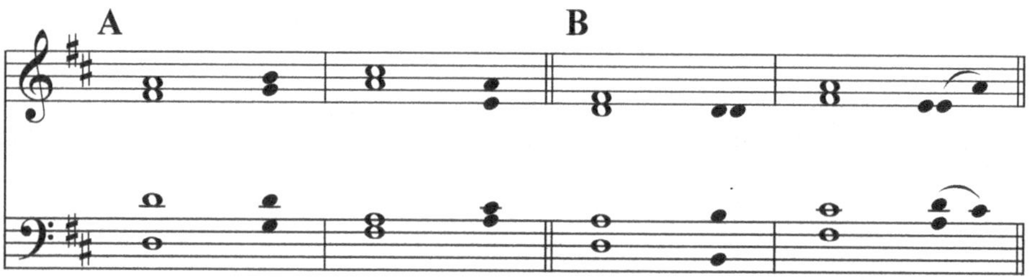

A 1 I love the LORD, because he has heard the voice of my supplication, *
because he has inclined his ear to me whenever I called upon him.

A 2 The cords of death entangled me;
the grip of the grave took hold of me; *
I came to grief and sorrow.

B 3 Then I called upon the Name of the LORD: *
"O LORD, I pray you, save my life." [ANT.]

A 4 Gracious is the LORD and righteous; *
our God is full of compassion.

A 5 The LORD watches over the innocent; *
I was brought very low, and he helped me.

B 6 Turn again to your rest, O my soul, *
for the LORD has treated you well. [ANT.]

7 For you have rescued my life from death, *
my eyes from tears, and my feet from stumbling.

8 I will walk in the presence of the LORD *
in the land of the living. [ANT.]

RCL Saturday in Easter Week ABC Psalm 118: 14–18

based on "Gelobt sei Gott" (H82–205)

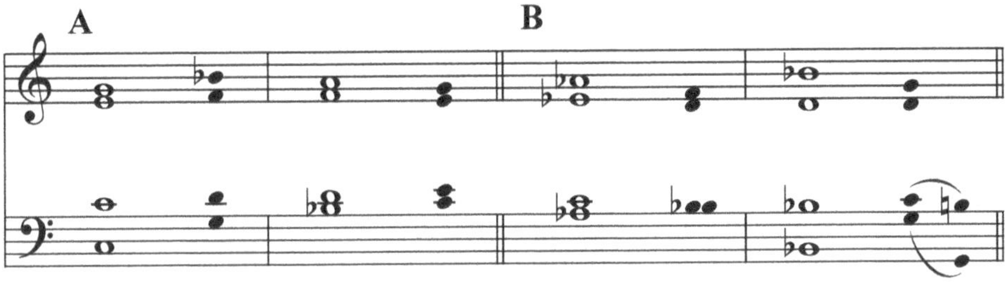

A 14 The LORD is my strength and my song, *
and he has become my salvation.
A 15 There is a sound of exultation and victory *
in the tents of the righteous:
B 16 "The right hand of the LORD has triumphed! *
the right hand of the LORD is exalted!
the right hand of the LORD has triumphed!" [ANT.]

17 I shall not die, but live, *
and declare the works of the LORD.
18 The LORD has punished me sorely, *
but he did not hand me over to death. [ANT.]

RCL Ascension Day ABC **Psalm 47**

based on "Truro" (H82–436)

1 Clap your hands, all you peoples; *
shout to God with a cry of joy.
2 For the LORD Most High is to be feared; *
he is the great King over all the earth. [ANT.]

3 He subdues the peoples under us, *
and the nations under our feet.
4 He chooses our inheritance for us, *
the pride of Jacob whom he loves. [ANT.]

6 Sing praises to God, sing praises; *
sing praises to our King, sing praises.
7 For God is King of all the earth; *
sing praises with all your skill. [ANT.]

A 8 God reigns over the nations; *
God sits upon his holy throne.
A 9 The nobles of the peoples have gathered together *
with the people of the God of Abraham.
B 10 The rulers of the earth belong to God, *
and he is highly exalted. [ANT.]

RCL Ascension Day ABC **Psalm 93**

based on "Hanover" (H82–388)

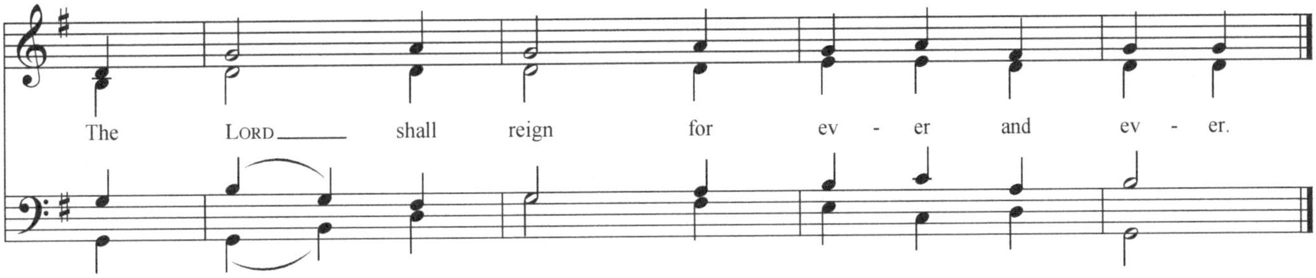

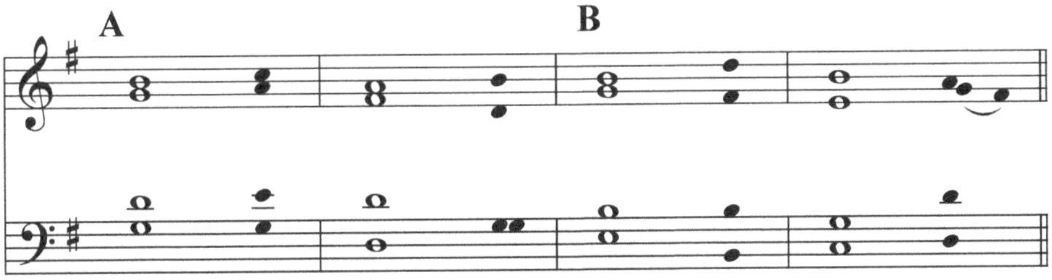

A 1 The LORD is King;
he has put on splendid apparel; *
the LORD has put on his apparel
and girded himself with strength.
A 2 He has made the whole world so sure *
that it cannot be moved;
B 3 Ever since the world began, your throne has been established; *
you are from everlasting. [ANT.]

A 4 The waters have lifted up, O LORD,
the waters have lifted up their voice; *
the waters have lifted up their pounding waves.
A 5 Mightier than the sound of many waters,
mightier than the breakers of the sea, *
mightier is the LORD who dwells on high.
B 6 Your testimonies are very sure, *
and holiness adorns your house, O LORD,
for ever and for evermore. [ANT.]

RCL Vigil of Pentecost ABC Psalm 33: 12–22

based on "Adoro devote" (H82–314)

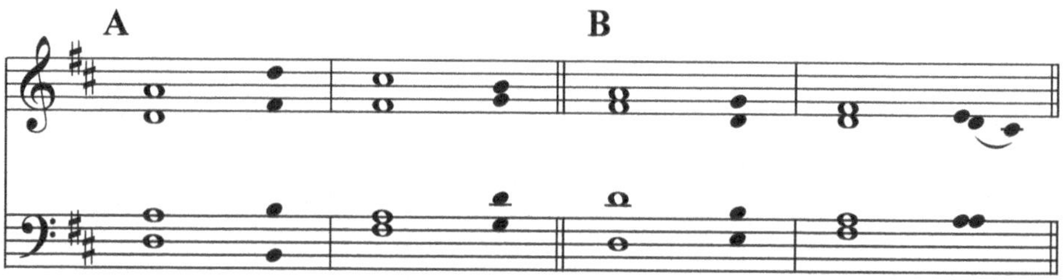

A 12 Happy is the nation whose God is the LORD! *
happy the people he has chosen to be his own!
B 13 The LORD looks down from heaven, *
and beholds all the people in the world.
A 14 From where he sits enthroned he turns his gaze *
on all who dwell on the earth.
B 15 He fashions all the hearts of them *
and understands all their works. [ANT.]

16 There is no king that can be saved by a mighty army;
a strong man is not delivered by his great strength.
17 The horse is a vain hope for deliverance; *
or all its strength it cannot save. [ANT.]

18 Behold, the eye of the LORD is upon those who fear him, *
on those who wait upon his love,
19 To pluck their lives from death, *
and to feed them in time of famine. [ANT.]

A 20 Our soul waits for the LORD; *
he is our help and our shield.
A 21 Indeed, our heart rejoices in him, *
for in his holy Name we put our trust.
B 22 Let your loving-kindness, O LORD, be upon us, *
as we have put our trust in you. [ANT.]

RCL Vigil of Pentecost ABC Canticle 13

based on "Foundation" (H82–636)

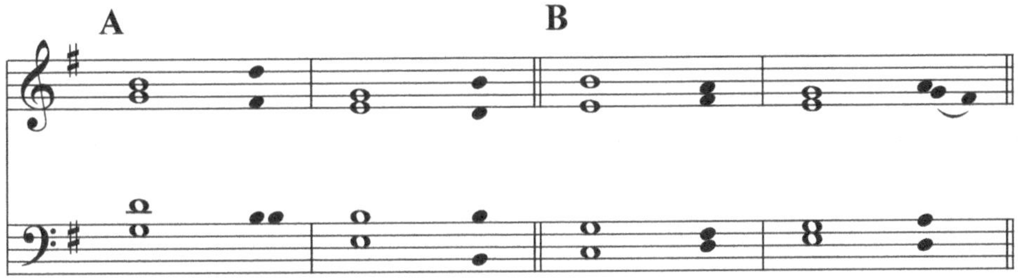

1 Glory to you, Lord God of our fathers; *
you are worthy of praise; glory to you.
2 Glory to you for the radiance of your holy Name; *
we will praise you and highly exalt you for ever. [ANT.]

3 Glory to you in the splendor of your temple; *
on the throne of your majesty, glory to you.
4 Glory to you, seated between the Cherubim; *
we will praise you and highly exalt you for ever. [ANT.]

5 Glory to you, beholding the depths; *
in the high vault of heaven, glory to you.
6 Glory to you, Father, Son, and Holy Spirit; *
we will praise you and highly exalt you for ever. [ANT.]

RCL Vigil of Pentecost ABC Psalm 130

based on "Pange lingua" (H82–166)

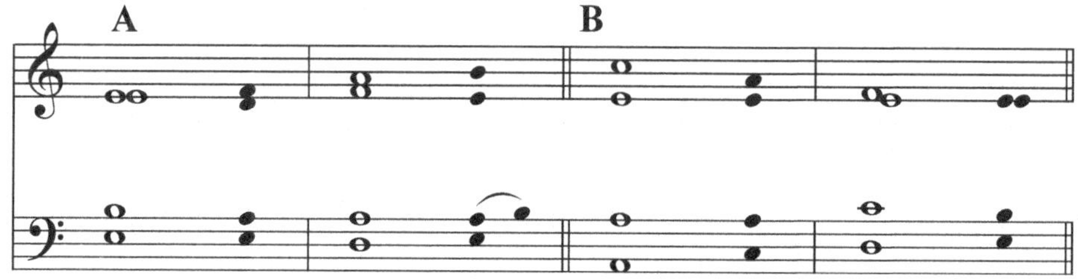

A 1 Out of the depths have I called to you, O LORD;
LORD, hear my voice; *
let your ears consider well the voice of my supplication.
A 2 If you, LORD, were to note what is done amiss, *
O LORD, who could stand?
B 3 For there is forgiveness with you; *
therefore you shall be feared. [ANT.]

4 I wait for the LORD; my soul waits for him; *
in his word is my hope.
5 My soul waits for the LORD,
more than watchmen for the morning, *
more than watchmen for the morning. [ANT.]

6 O Israel, wait for the LORD, *
for with the LORD there is mercy;
7 With him there is plenteous redemption, *
and he shall redeem Israel from all their sins. [ANT.]

RCL Vigil of Pentecost ABC   Canticle 9

based on "Lasst uns erfreuen" (H82–400)

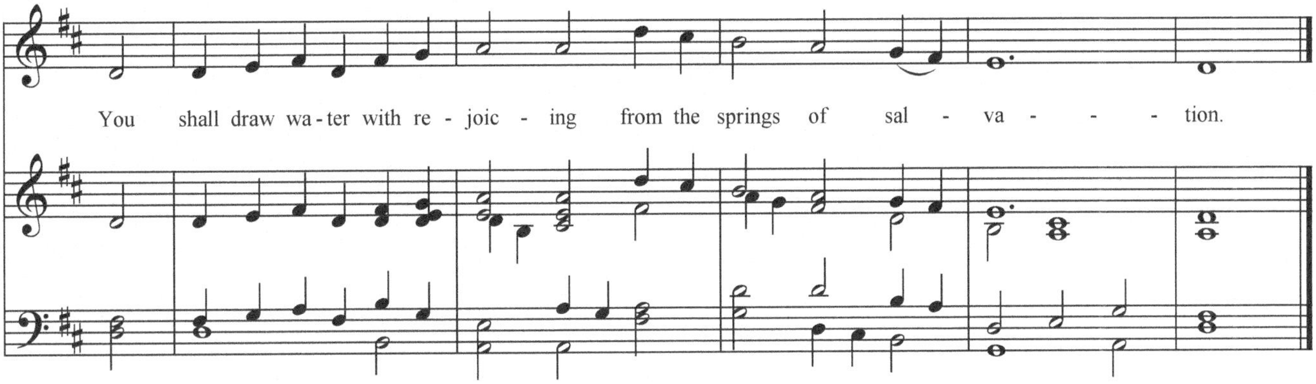

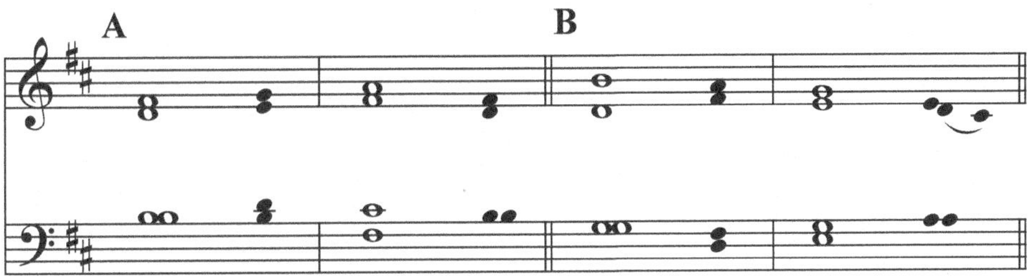

1 Surely, it is God who saves me; *
  I will trust in him and not be afraid.
2 For the Lord is my stronghold and my sure defense, *
  and he will be my Savior. [ANT.]

4 And on that day you shall say, *
  Give thanks to the Lord and call upon his Name;
5 Make his deeds known among the peoples; *
  see that they remember that his Name is exalted. [ANT.]

6 Sing the praises of the Lord, for he has done great things, *
  and this is known in all the world.
7 Cry aloud, inhabitants of Zion, ring out your joy, *
  for the great one in the midst of you is the Holy One of Israel. [ANT.]

RCL Vigil of Pentecost ABC Psalm 104: 25–32

based on "Veni Creator Spiritus" (H82–502, 504)

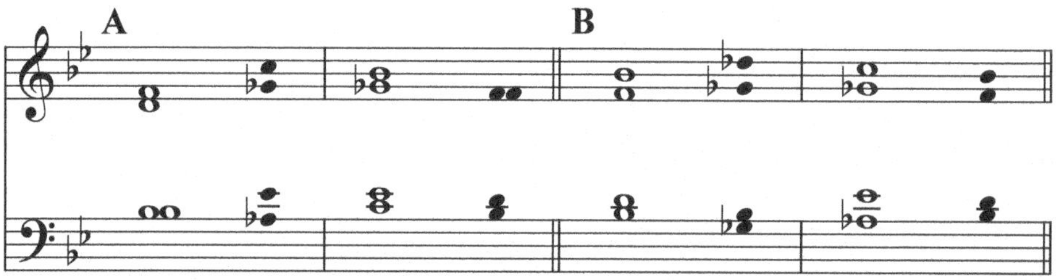

25 O Lord, how manifold are your works! *
in wisdom you have made them all;
the earth is full of your creatures.
26 Yonder is the great and wide sea
with its living things too many to number, *
creatures both small and great. [ANT.]

27 There move the ships,
and there is that Leviathan, *
which you have made for the sport of it.
28 All of them look to you *
to give them their food in due season. [ANT.]

29 You give it to them; they gather it; *
you open your hand, and they are filled with good things.
30 You hide your face, and they are terrified; *
you take away their breath,
and they die and return to their dust. [ANT.]

31 You send forth your Spirit, and they are created; *
and so you renew the face of the earth.
32 May the glory of the Lord endure for ever; *
may the Lord rejoice in all his works. [ANT.]

RCL Pentecost ABC Psalm 104: 25–35, 37

based on "Veni Creator Spiritus" (H82–502, 504)

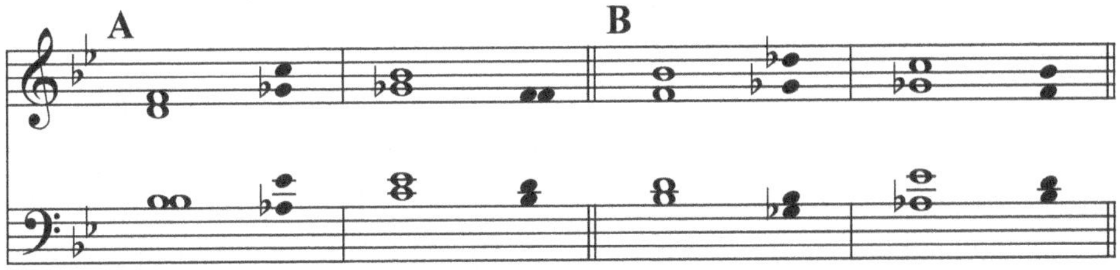

25 O LORD, how manifold are your works! *
in wisdom you have made them all;
the earth is full of your creatures.
26 Yonder is the great and wide sea
with its living things too many to number, *
creatures both small and great. [ANT.]

27 There move the ships,
and there is that Leviathan, *
which you have made for the sport of it.
28 All of them look to you *
to give them their food in due season. [ANT.]

29 You give it to them; they gather it; *
you open your hand, and they are filled with good things.
30 You hide your face, and they are terrified; *
you take away their breath,
and they die and return to their dust. [ANT.]

A 31 You send forth your Spirit, and they are created; *
and so you renew the face of the earth.
A 32 May the glory of the LORD endure for ever; *
may the LORD rejoice in all his works.
B 33 He looks at the earth and it trembles; *
he touches the mountains and they smoke. [ANT.]

A 34 I will sing to the LORD as long as I live; *
I will praise my God while I have my being.
A 35 May these words of mine please him; *
I will rejoice in the LORD.
B 37 Bless the LORD, O my soul. *
Hallelujah! [ANT.]

APPENDIX

RCL Advent 1A Psalm 122

RCL Advent 2A Psalm 72: 1–8, 18–19

RCL Advent 3A Psalm 146: 4–9

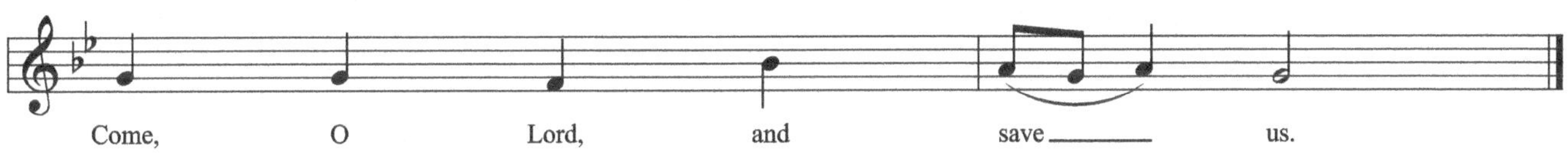

RCL Advent 3A Canticle 15

RCL Advent 4A Psalm 80: 1–7, 16–18

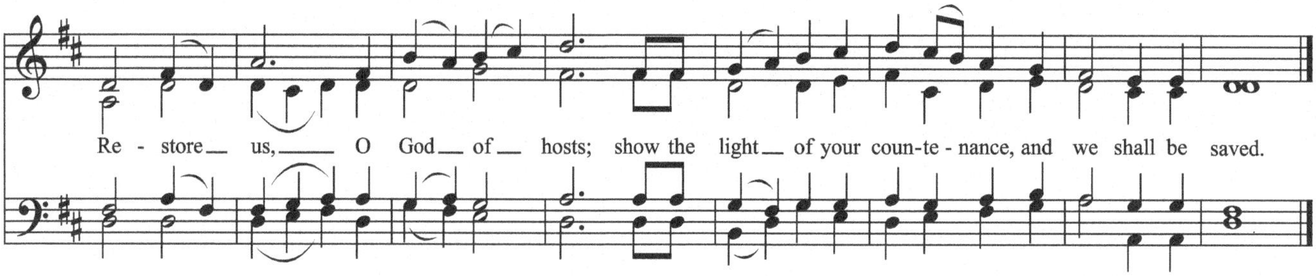

From *A HymnTune Psalter, Revised Common Lectionary Edition* © 2007 by Carl P. Daw, Jr. and Kevin R. Hackett. Church Publishing Incorporated.

RCL Epiphany 2A Psalm 40: 1–12

From *A HymnTune Psalter, Revised Common Lectionary Edition* © 2007 by Carl P. Daw, Jr. and Kevin R. Hackett. Church Publishing Incorporated.

RCL Epiphany 3A Psalm 27: 1, 5–13

From *A HymnTune Psalter, Revised Common Lectionary Edition* © 2007 by Carl P. Daw, Jr. and Kevin R. Hackett. Church Publishing Incorporated.

RCL Epiphany 4A Psalm 15

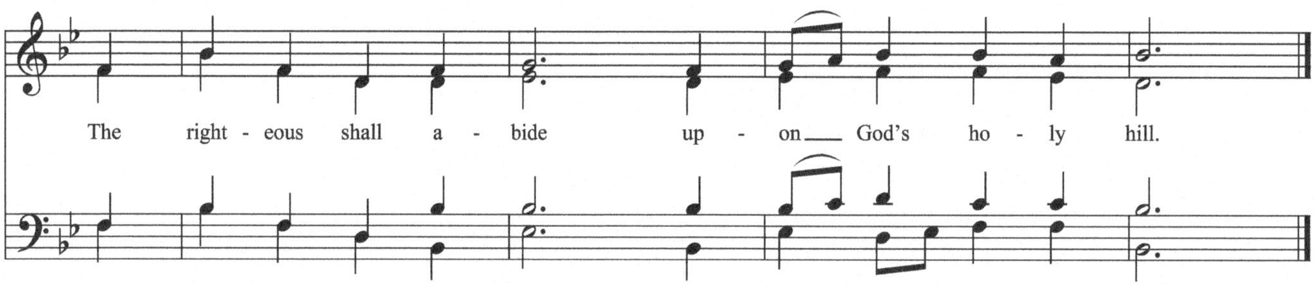

From *A HymnTune Psalter, Revised Common Lectionary Edition* © 2007 by Carl P. Daw, Jr. and Kevin R. Hackett. Church Publishing Incorporated.

RCL Epiphany 5A Psalm 112: 1–9 (10)

From *A HymnTune Psalter, Revised Common Lectionary Edition*

RCL Epiphany 6A Psalm 119: 1–8

From *A HymnTune Psalter, Revised Common Lectionary Edition*

RCL Epiphany 7A Psalm 119: 33–40

From *A HymnTune Psalter, Revised Common Lectionary Edition*

RCL Epiphany 8A Psalm 131

From *A HymnTune Psalter, Revised Common Lectionary Edition*

RCL Epiphany Last A Psalm 2

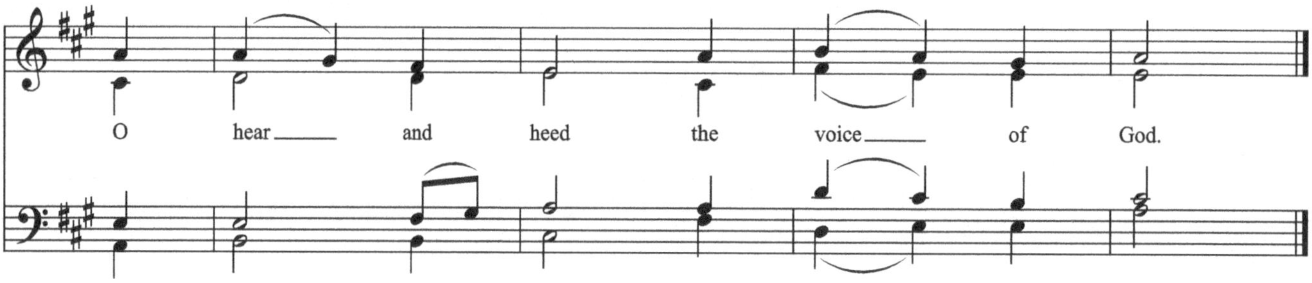

RCL Epiphany Last A Psalm 99

RCL Lent 1A Psalm 32

RCL Lent 2A Psalm 121

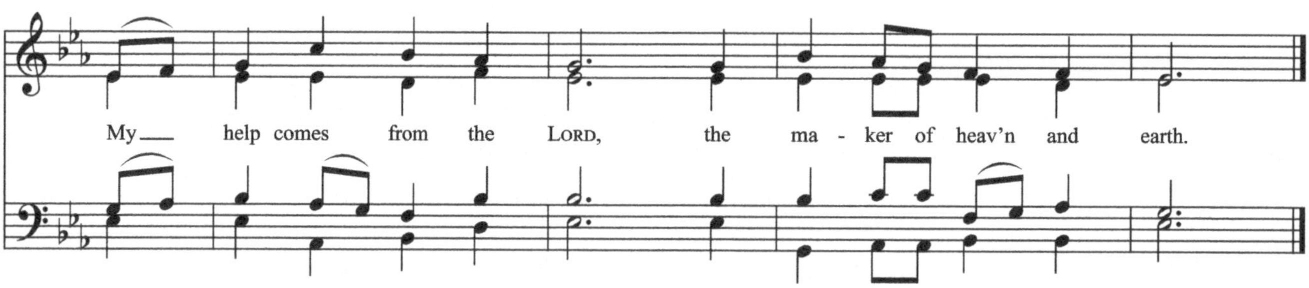

RCL Lent 3A Psalm 95

RCL Lent 4A Psalm 23

RCL Lent 5A Psalm 130

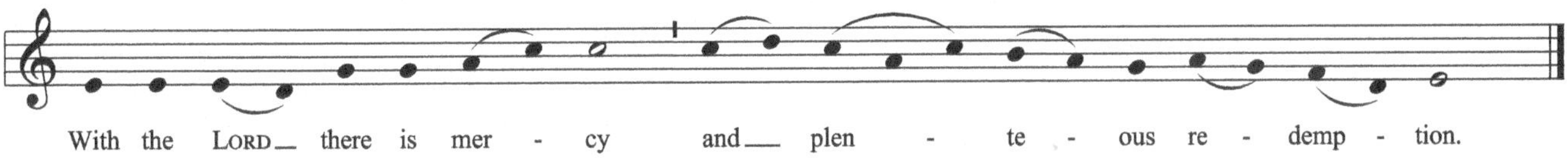

RCL Easter 2A **Psalm 16**

RCL Easter 3A **Psalm 116: 1–3, 10–17**

RCL Easter 4A **Psalm 23**

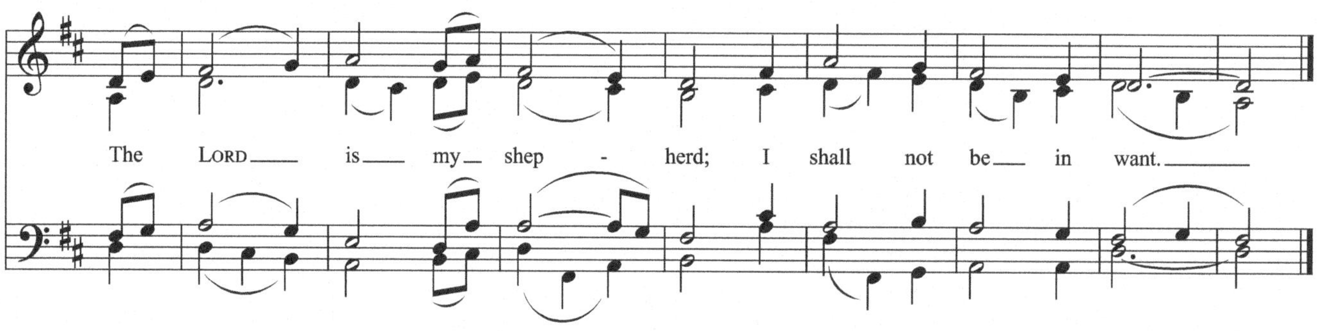

RCL Easter 5A **Psalm 31: 1–5, 15–16**

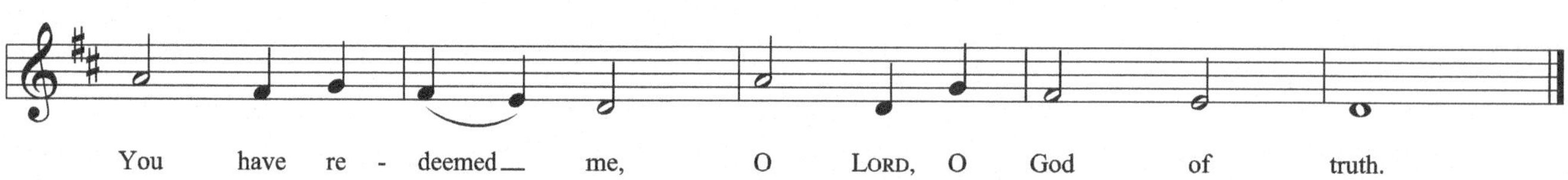

RCL Easter 6A Psalm 66: 7–18

RCL Easter 7A Psalm 68: 1–10, 33–36

RCL Advent 1B Psalm 80: 1–7, 16–18

RCL Advent 2B Psalm 85: 1–2, 8–13

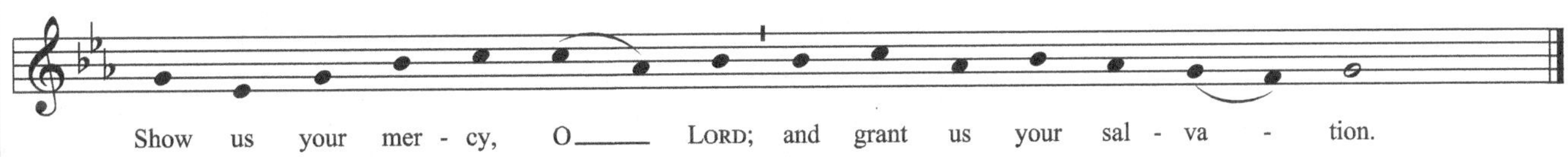

RCL Advent 3B Psalm 126

RCL Advent 3B Canticle 15

RCL Advent 4B Canticle 15

RCL Advent 4B Psalm 89: 1–4, 19–26

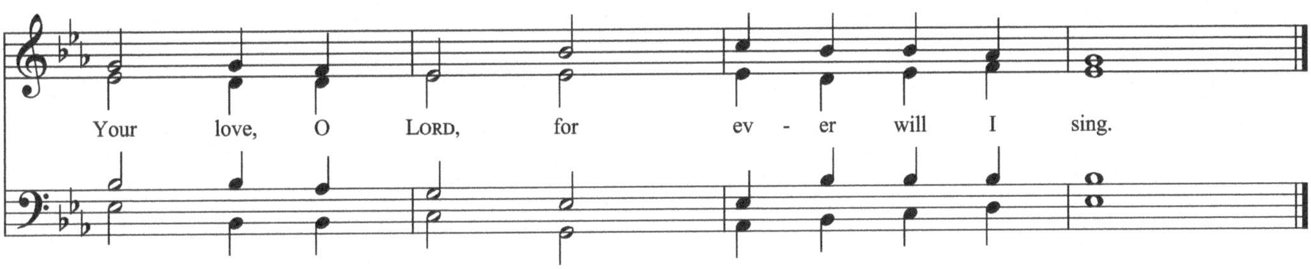

RCL Epiphany 2B Psalm 139: 1–5, 12–17

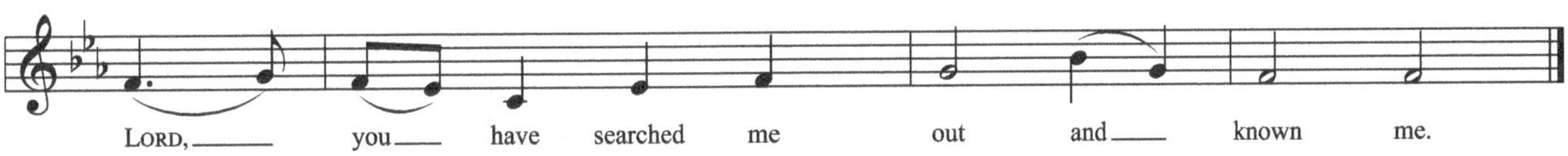

RCL Epiphany 3B Psalm 62: 6–14

RCL Epiphany 4B Psalm 111

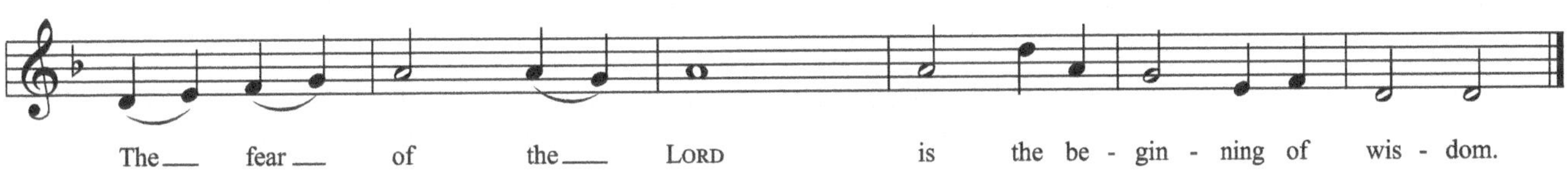

RCL Epiphany 5B Psalm 147: 1–12, 21c

From *A HymnTune Psalter, Revised Common Lectionary Edition* © 2007 by Carl P. Daw, Jr. and Kevin R. Hackett. Church Publishing Incorporated.

RCL Epiphany 6B Psalm 30

From *A HymnTune Psalter, Revised Common Lectionary Edition* © 2007 by Carl P. Daw, Jr. and Kevin R. Hackett. Church Publishing Incorporated.

RCL Epiphany 7B Psalm 41

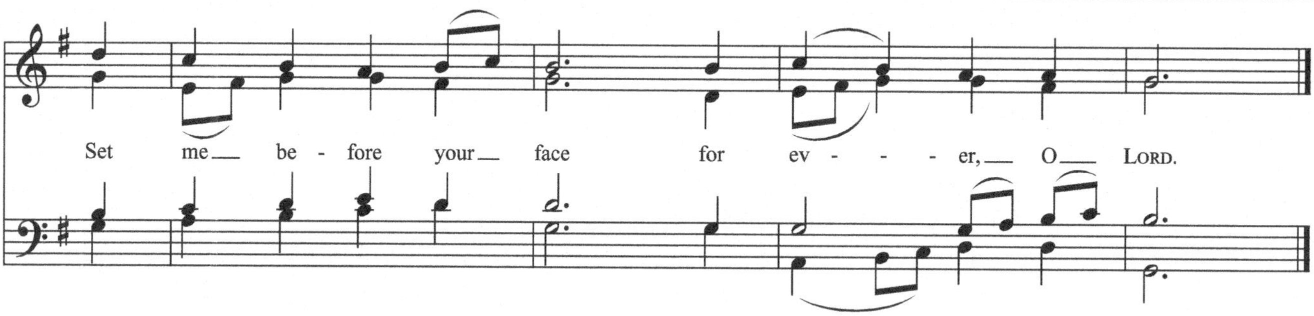

From *A HymnTune Psalter, Revised Common Lectionary Edition* © 2007 by Carl P. Daw, Jr. and Kevin R. Hackett. Church Publishing Incorporated.

RCL Epiphany 8B   Psalm 103: 1–13, 22

RCL Epiphany Last   Psalm 50: 1–6

RCL Lent 1B   Psalm 25: 1–9

RCL Lent 2B   Psalm 22: 22–30

RCL Lent 3B Psalm 19

RCL Lent 4B Psalm 107: 1–3, 17–22

RCL Lent 5B Psalm 51: 1–13

RCL Lent 5B Psalm 119: 9–16

RCL Easter 2B Psalm 133

RCL Easter 3B Psalm 4

RCL Easter 4B Psalm 23

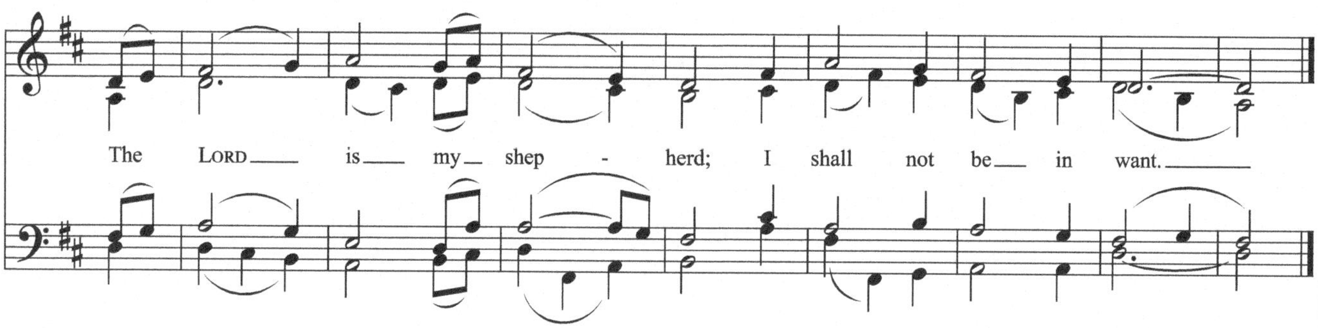

RCL Easter 5B Psalm 22: 24–30

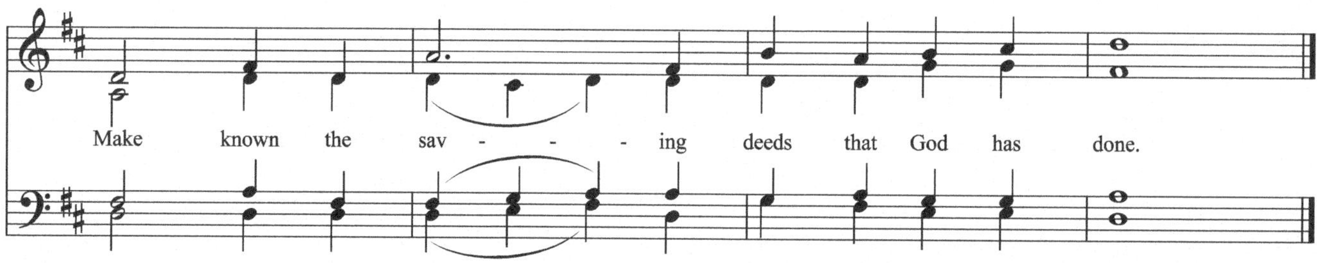

RCL Easter 6B Psalm 98

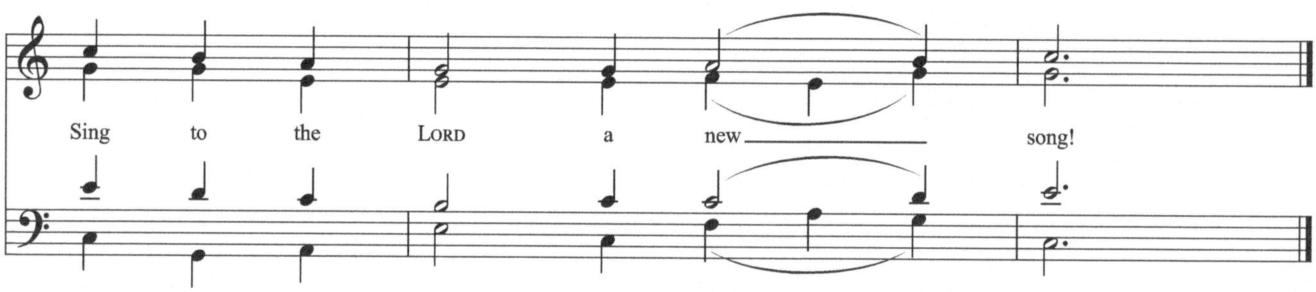

RCL Easter 7B Psalm 1

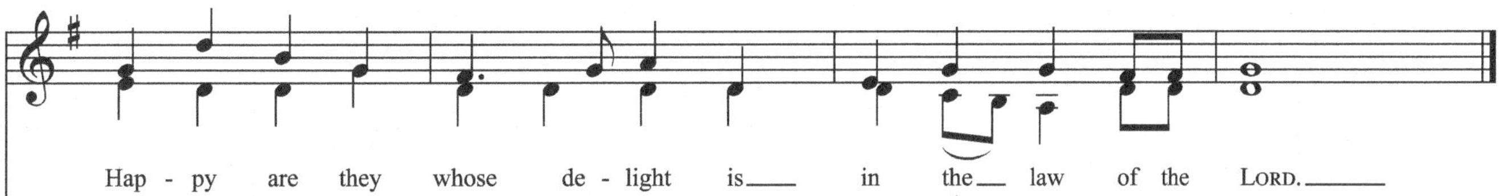

RCL Advent 1C Psalm 25: 1–9

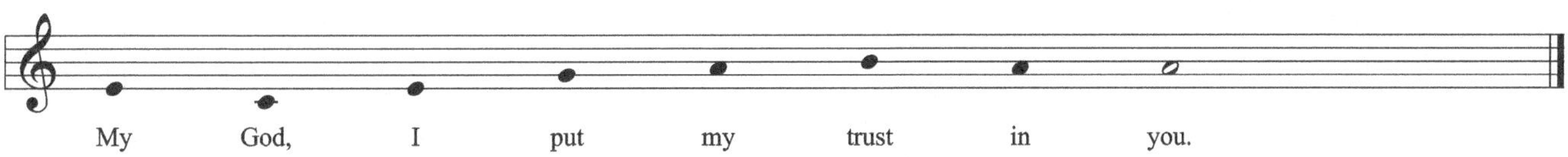

RCL Advent 2C Canticle 16

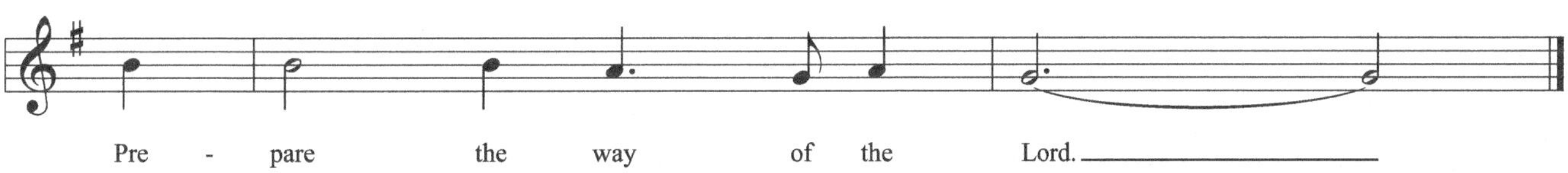

RCL Advent 3C Canticle 9

RCL Advent 4C Canticle 15

RCL Advent 4C Psalm 80: 1–7

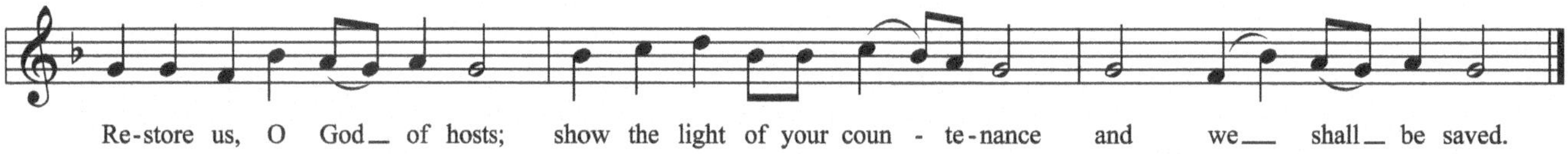

RCL Epiphany 2C Psalm 36: 5–10

RCL Epiphany 3C Psalm 19

RCL Epiphany 4C **Psalm 71: 1–6**

RCL Epiphany 5C **Psalm 138**

RCL Epiphany 6C **Psalm 1**

RCL Epiphany 7C **Psalm 37: 1–12, 41–42**

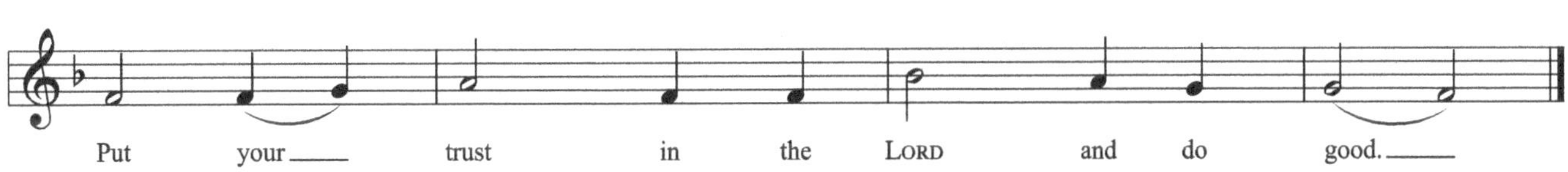

RCL Epiphany 8C   Psalm 92: 1–4, 11–14

From *A HymnTune Psalter, Revised Common Lectionary Edition* © 2007 by Carl P. Daw, Jr. and Kevin R. Hackett. Church Publishing Incorporated.

RCL Epiphany Last C   Psalm 99

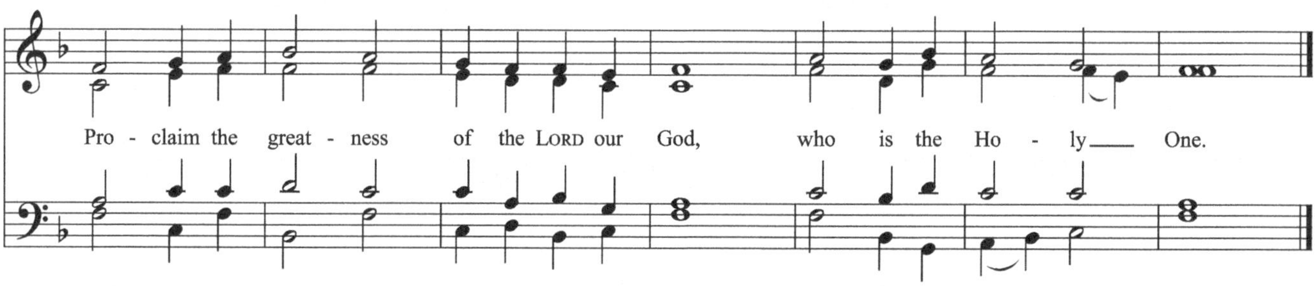

From *A HymnTune Psalter, Revised Common Lectionary Edition* © 2007 by Carl P. Daw, Jr. and Kevin R. Hackett. Church Publishing Incorporated.

RCL Lent 1C   Psalm 91: 1–2, 9–16

From *A HymnTune Psalter, Revised Common Lectionary Edition* © 2007 by Carl P. Daw, Jr. and Kevin R. Hackett. Church Publishing Incorporated.

RCL Lent 2C Psalm 27

RCL Lent 3C Psalm 63: 1–8

RCL Lent 4C Psalm 32

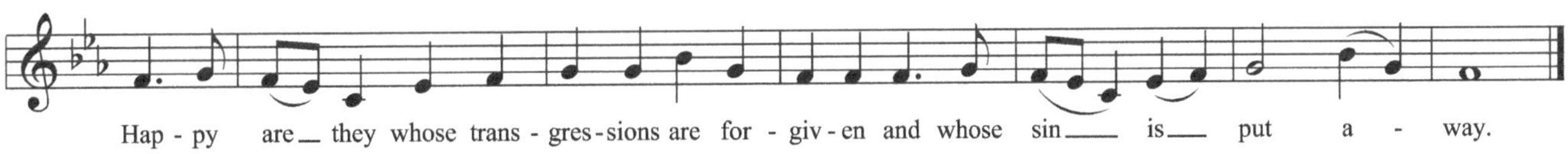

RCL Lent 5C Psalm 126

RCL Easter 2C Psalm 118: 14–29

RCL Easter 2C Psalm 150

RCL Easter 3C Psalm 30

RCL Easter 4C Psalm 23

RCL Easter 5C Psalm 148

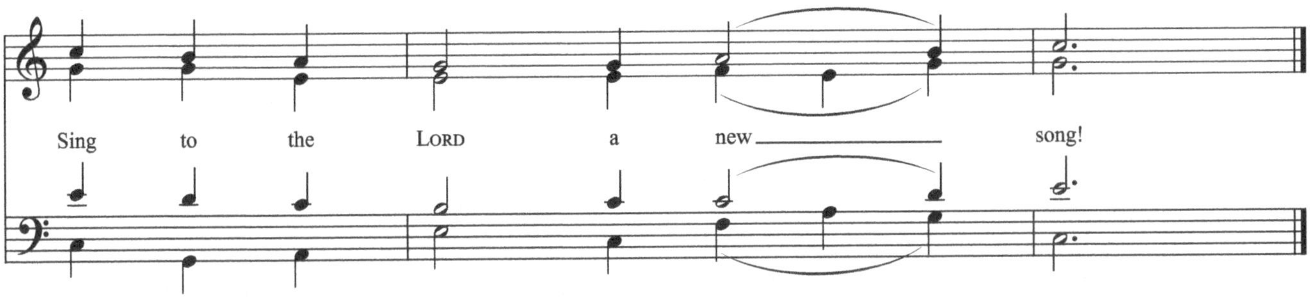

RCL Easter 6C Psalm 67

RCL Easter 7C Psalm 97

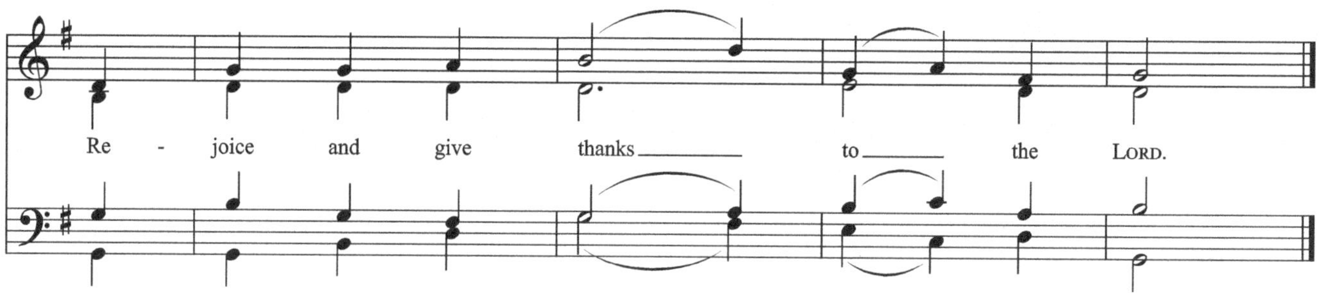

RCL Christmas Day I ABC Psalm 96

RCL Christmas Day II ABC Psalm 97

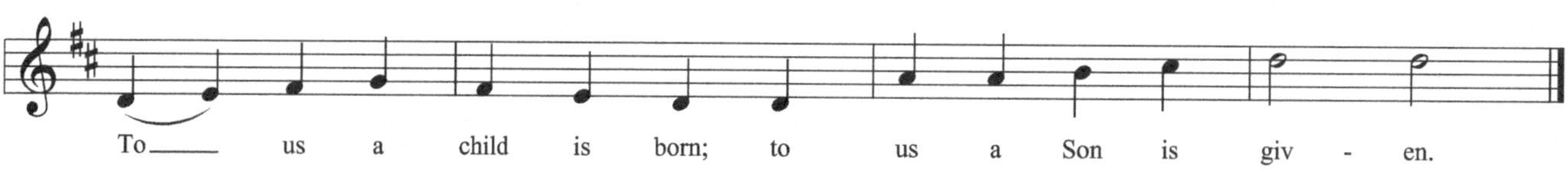

RCL Christmas Day III ABC Psalm 98

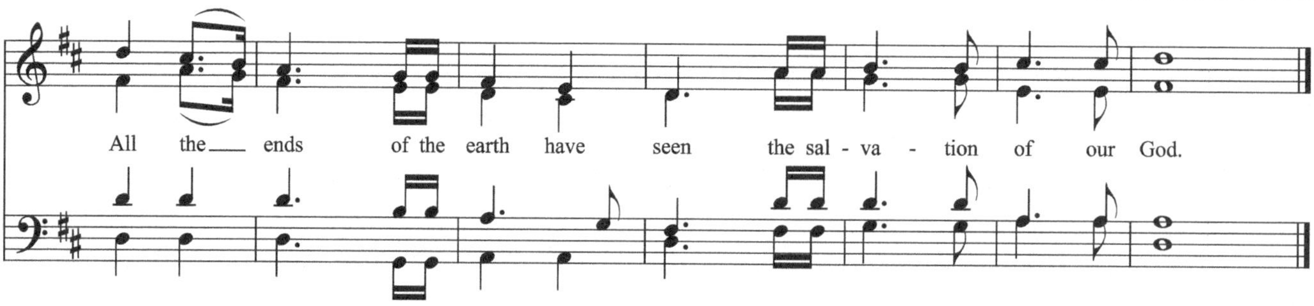

RCL Christmas 1 ABC Psalm 147: 13–21

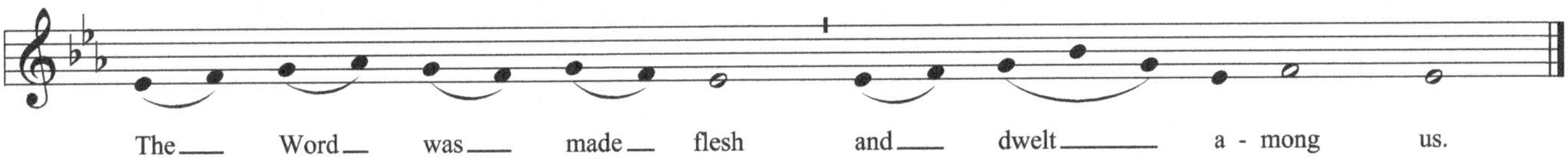

RCL Holy Name ABC Psalm 8

RCL Christmas 2 ABC Psalm 84: 1–8

RCL Epiphany ABC Psalm 72: 1–7, 10–14

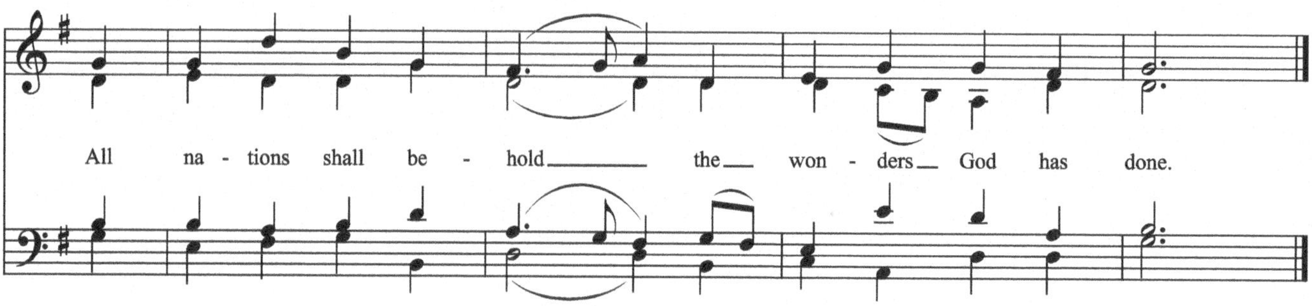

RCL Epiphany 1 ABC Psalm 29

RCL Presentation ABC Psalm 84

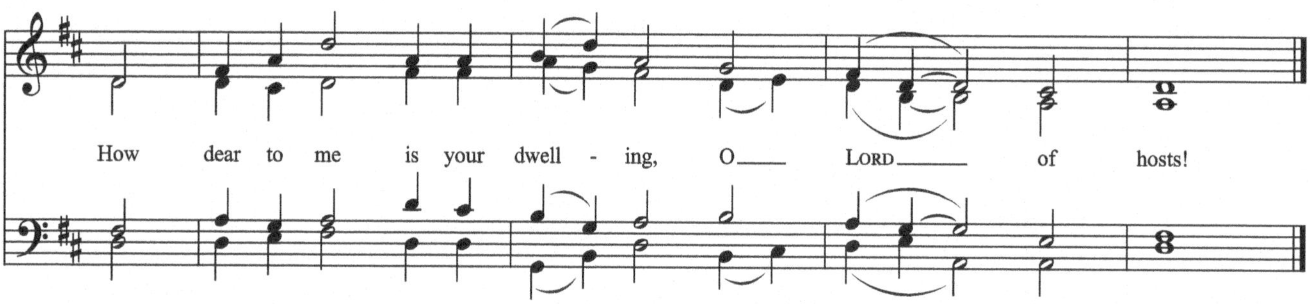

RCL Presentation ABC Psalm 24:7–10

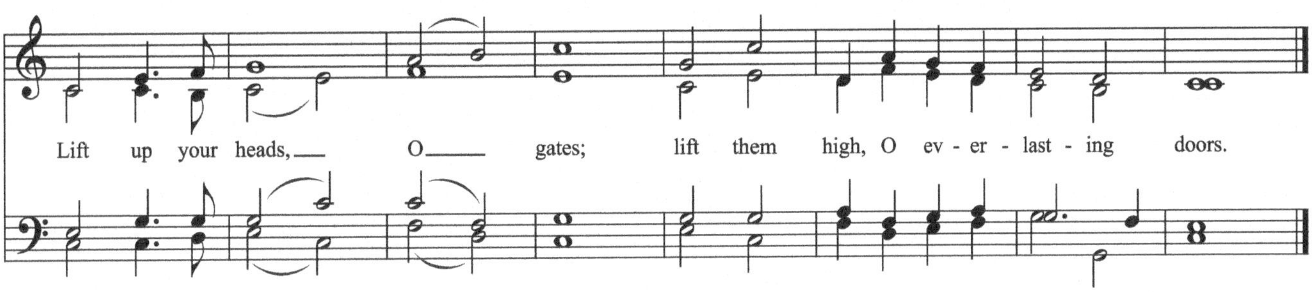

RCL Ash Wednesday ABC Psalm 103: 8–14

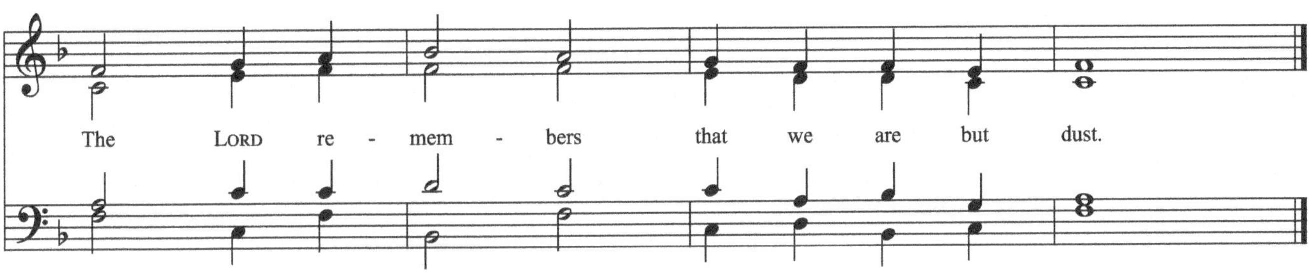

RCL Palm Sunday–Liturgy of the Palms ABC   Psalm 118: 1–2, 19–29

RCL Palm Sunday ABC   Psalm 31: 9–16

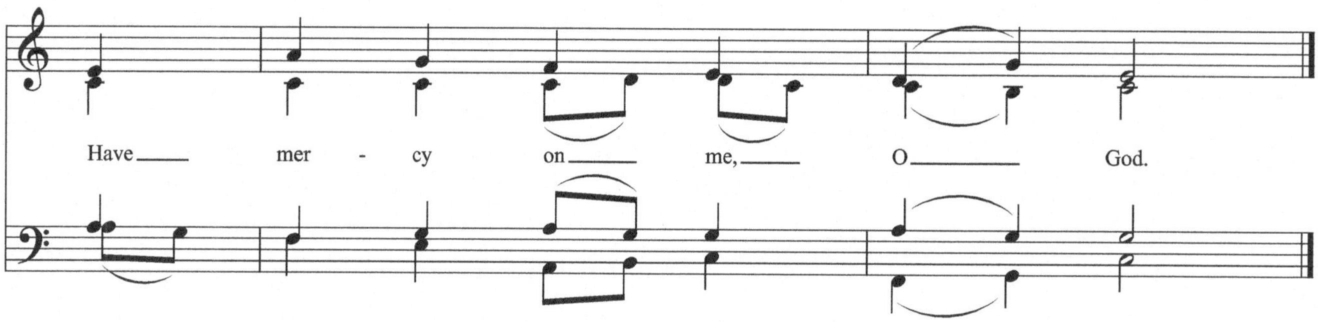

RCL Monday in Holy Week ABC   Psalm 36: 5–11

RCL Tuesday in Holy Week ABC   Psalm 71: 1–14

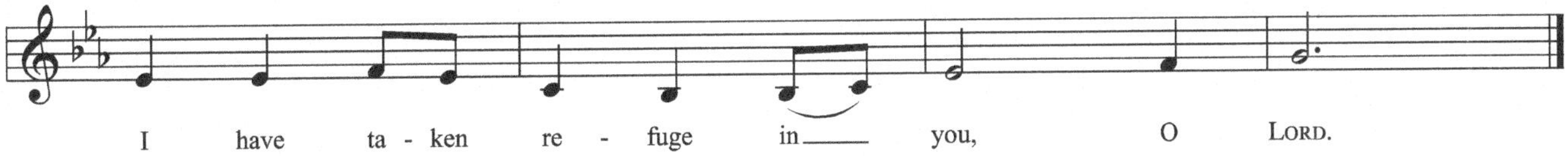

RCL Wednesday in Holy Week ABC   Psalm 70

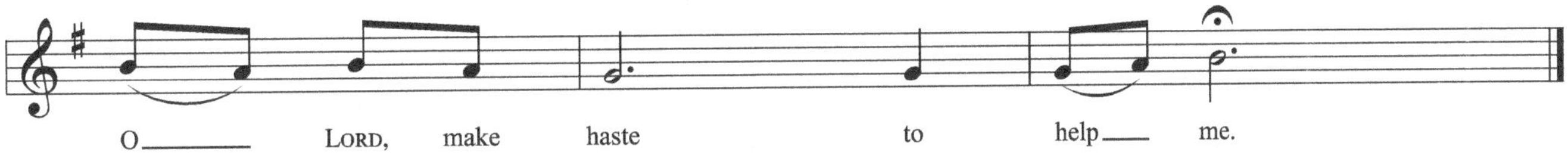

RCL Maundy Thursday ABC   Psalm 116: 1, 10–17

RCL Good Friday ABC   Psalm 22

RCL Holy Saturday ABC Psalm 31: 1–4, 15–16

RCL Great Vigil of Easter ABC Psalm 136: 1–9, 23–26

RCL Great Vigil of Easter ABC Psalm 46

RCL Great Vigil of Easter ABC Psalm 16

RCL Great Vigil of Easter ABC Canticle 8

RCL Great Vigil of Easter ABC Canticle 9

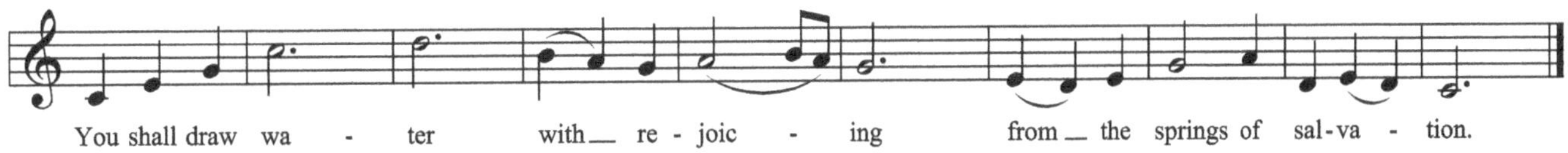

RCL Great Vigil of Easter ABC Psalm 19

RCL Great Vigil of Easter ABC Psalms 42 & 43

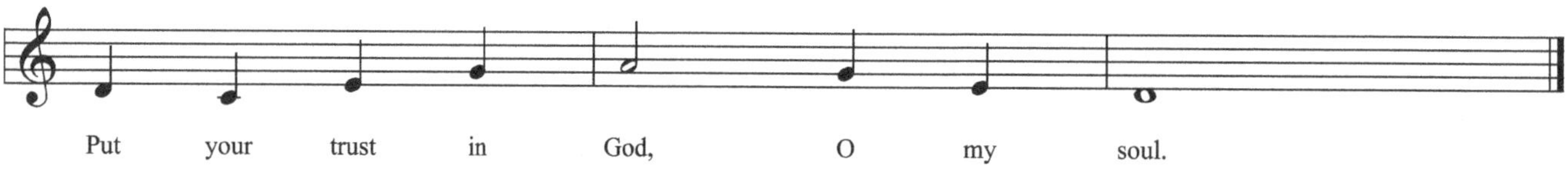

RCL Great Vigil of Easter ABC Psalm 143

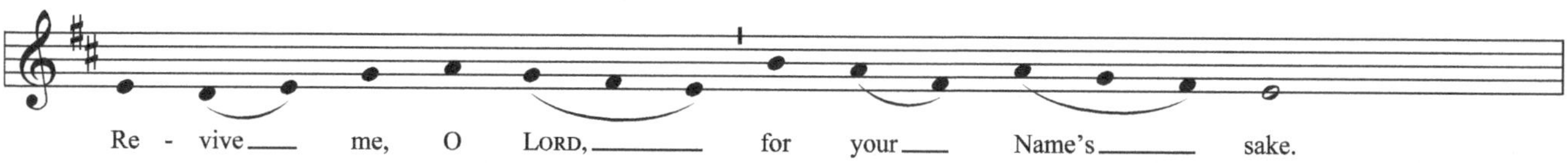

RCL Great Vigil of Easter ABC Psalm 98

RCL Easter Day (Early) ABC **Psalm 114**

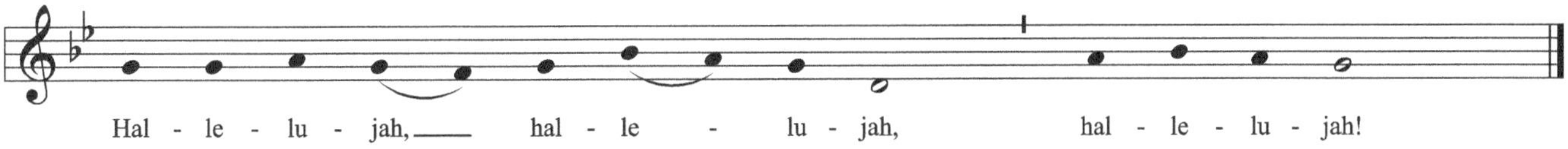

RCL Easter Day ABC (Principal Service) **Psalm 118: 1–2, 14–24**

RCL Easter Day (Evening) ABC **Psalm 114**

RCL Monday in Easter Week ABC **Psalm 16: 8–11**

RCL Monday-Saturday in Easter Week ABC **Psalm 118: 19–24**

RCL Tuesday in Easter Week ABC **Psalm 33: 18–22**

RCL Wednesday in Easter Week ABC **Psalm 105: 1–8**

RCL Thursday in Easter Week ABC **Psalm 8**

RCL Friday in Easter Week ABC Psalm 116: 1–8

RCL Saturday in Easter Week ABC Psalm 118: 14–18

RCL Ascension Day ABC Psalm 47

RCL Ascension Day ABC **Psalm 93**

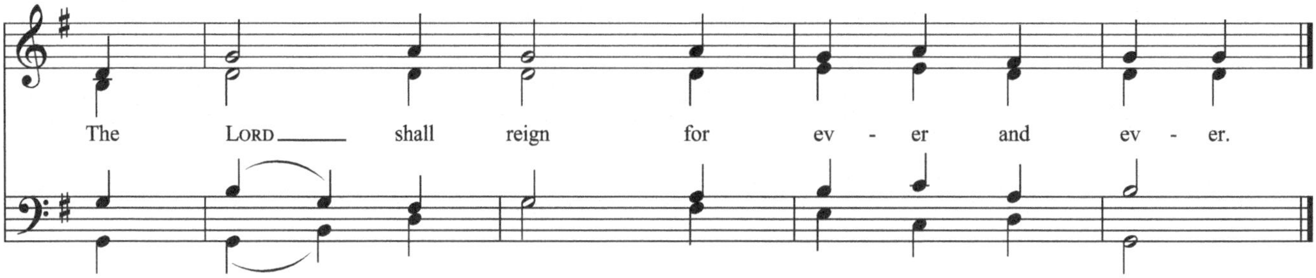

RCL Vigil of Pentecost ABC **Psalm 33: 12–22**

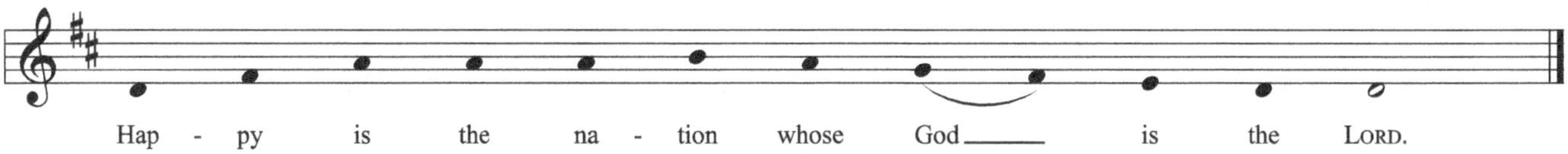

RCL Vigil of Pentecost ABC **Canticle 13**

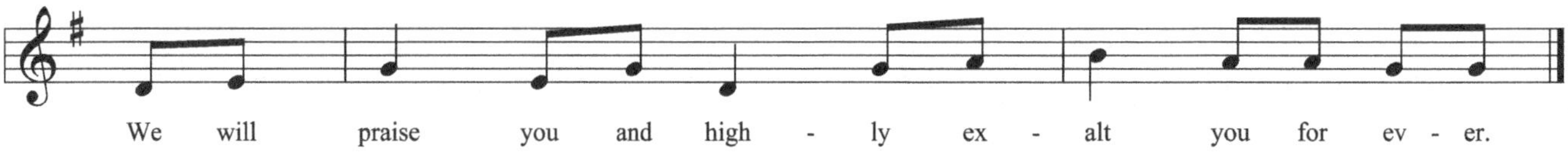

RCL Vigil of Pentecost ABC **Psalm 130**

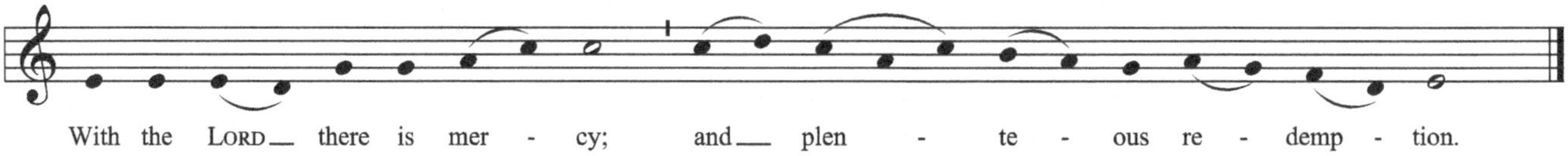

RCL Vigil of Pentecost ABC Canticle 9

RCL Vigil of Pentecost ABC Psalm 104: 25–32

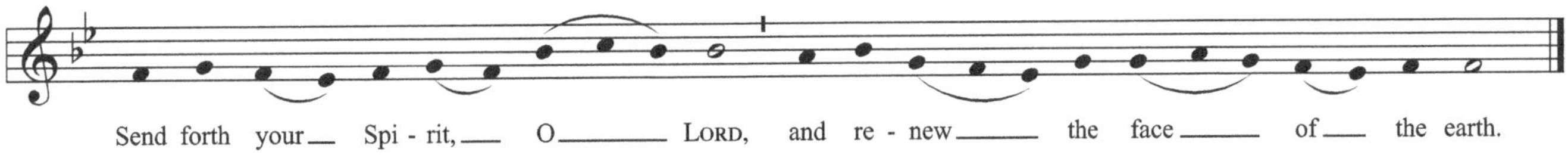

RCL Pentecost ABC Psalm 104: 25–35, 37

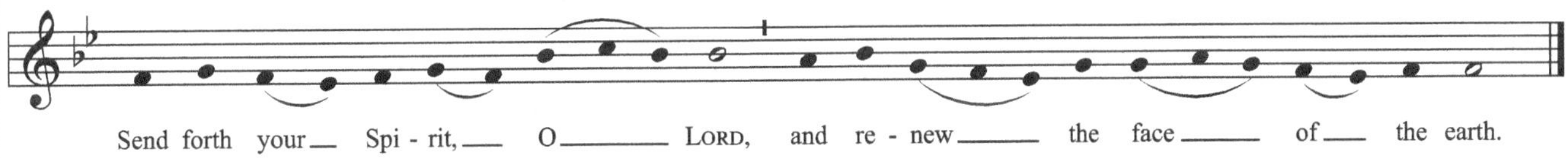